A G... to the New World

*why mutual guarantee
is the key to our recovery
from the global crisis*

ARI
Publishers

Michael Laitman, PhD
&
Anatloy Ulianov, PhD

A Guide to the New World: why mutual guarantee
is the key to our recovery from the global crisis

Copyright © 2012 by Michael Laitman

Published by ARI Publishers
www.ariresearch.org   info@ariresearch.org
1057 Steeles Avenue West, Suite 532, Toronto, ON, M2R 3X1, Canada
2009 85th Street #51, Brooklyn, New York, 11214, USA

Printed in Canada

ISBN: 978-1-897448-72-4

Library of Congress Control Number: 2012905804

Translation: Chaim Ratz
Associate Editor: Mary Miesem
Copy Editor: Claire Gerus
Layout: Baruch Khovov
Cover: Inna Smirnova
Executive Editor: Chaim Ratz
Publishing and Post Production: Uri Laitman

FIRST EDITION: JANUARY 2013
First printing

Foreword 5
The Structure of the Book 7

PART ONE: REVOLUTION OF THE HEART 13
CHAPTER 1: A New World 11
CHAPTER 2: Nature and Us 25
CHAPTER 3: The Practical Way 41
CHAPTER 4: Social Justice 73

PART TWO: BUILDING A NEW SOCIETY 83
Crisis and Opportunity 85
Natural Development 91
Social Solidarity 95

APPENDICES 99
PREVIOUS PUBLICATIONS BY THE ARI INSTITUTE 101
    We, We, We 101
    The Road to Social Justice 107
    Toward Mutual Commitment 110
    The Benefits of the New Economy...........116
    The Mutual Guarantee – Educational Agenda.......131
ABOUT THE ARI INSTITUTE 139
FURTHER READING 149

Notes 152

FOREWORD

The social unrest that began in 2011 caught on like a global bushfire, demanding equality, social justice, just distribution of income, and in some cases, democracy.

Why does 1% of the world population own 40% of the wealth? Why are education systems throughout the world producing unhappy and uneducated children? Why is there hunger? Why are costs of living rising when there is enough production of every staple to provide for everyone, with a surplus left over? Why are there still some countries where human dignity and social justice are nonexistent? And most of all, when and how will these wrongs be made right?

In 2011, these questions touched the hearts of hundreds of millions the world over, and people took to the streets. The cry for social justice has become a demand around which all can unite, regardless of race, religion, sex, or color, because we all long for a society where we can feel safe, trust our neighbors and our friends, and guarantee the future of our children. In such a society, all will care for all, and mutual guarantee—where all are guarantors of each other's well-being—will thrive.

But how can we achieve mutual guarantee? How do citizens become confident and secure, knowing that if they fall tomorrow, there will be someone to look after them?

The search for the answers to these complicated, worthwhile questions led to the decision to write this book. Yes, despite all the challenges, we believe that change is possible and that we can find a way to implement it. And precisely because of it, the book you are holding in your hands is a positive, *optimistic* one.

We now have a unique opportunity to achieve global transformation in a peaceful and pleasant manner, and this book tries to help us pave the way toward that goal.

THE STRUCTURE OF THE BOOK

The book is divided into two parts and indices.

PART 1:
The concept of mutual guarantee.

Chapter 1:
The emerging integral world.

Chapter 2:
How Nature fits into the concept of mutual guarantee.

Chapter 3:
Implementing the principles of mutual guarantee in society.

Chapter 4:
A new approach to the concept of social justice.

PART 2
"Building a New Society:" a recap and new perspectives on the principles presented in Part 1.

Indices
References to publications concerning society, economy, and education.

Part One

Revolution
of the Heart

A NEW WORLD

"We are all in one boat, one global economy. Our
fortunes rise together, and they fall together. ...We
have a collective responsibility—to bring about a
more stable and more prosperous world, a world
in which every person in every country can reach
their full potential."[1]

Christine Lagarde, Managing Director of
the International Monetary Fund (IMF)

T he worldwide unrest of 2011 irreversibly changed
the world. Millions of people took to the streets
in numerous countries on every continent,
from the Arab Spring through Occupy Wall Street.
Wherever the "social storm" hit, the demands for social
justice and equality resonated through the crowds
(with understandable variations among countries and
cultures). People began to demand solutions to their

problems; they wanted change. Often, people could not quite formulate their demands in words, but a deep sensation that they were being mistreated prompted them to act, to go out to the streets and protest, sometimes at the risk of their lives.

Why did these protests occur? Why did they occur at this point in time? Why did they happen with such synchrony, seeming to fuel one another? To understand how things work in a global age, we need to look at the state of humanity from a broad angle rather than consider each aspect in the state of humanity separately.

> "Historians will look back and say this was no ordinary time but a defining moment: an unprecedented period of global change, a time when one chapter ended and another began - for nations; for continents; for the whole world."[2]
>
> Gordon Brown, historian,
> former Prime Minister of the U.K. (2008)

Since the outbreak of the global crisis in 2008 it has become increasingly clear that we are at a historic tipping point. Divorce rates are constantly rising, and many people have no wish to marry or have a family.[3] Drug abuse is increasing,[4] and violence and crime continue, despite the fact that the U.S. prison population has more than doubled over the past 15 years.[5] The educational system is in collapse,[6] with institutions either offering poor schooling or education that's out of affordable range for most people.[7] Personal insecurity is so high that today there are more guns in the hands of citizens in America than there are citizens,[8] and the trend is growing.[9] In light of all this, it is no surprise that "nearly 40 percent of the people suffer mental illness."[10]

Until today, humanity had gradually advanced from generation to generation in the belief that our children would have a better life than our own. This gave us power and hope. But today, the future doesn't seem so bright.[11] It appears as if humanity has lost its way.

The primary indicator of our bewilderment concerning the future is the economic situation. Since 2008, the world has been in a prolonged economic crisis. Worse yet, the prospects of finding a way out of it seem dim. Nouriel Roubini, a leading economist and predictor of the global crisis, warned that we could be facing "Another Great Depression. Things are getting worse and the big difference between now and a few years ago is that this time around we're running out of policy bullets."[12]

Business magnate and investor, George Soros, also claims, "We are on the verge of an economic collapse."[13] And Sir Mervyn King, the current Governor of the Bank of England, concludes, "This is the most serious financial crisis we've seen, at least since the 1930s, if not ever."[14]

The continuous decline of the global economy is worrisome because it concerns more than our money. The economy is not a neutral network of industry, trade, and banking. More than anything, it reflects our own ambitions and desires, our relationships and the direction toward which we are headed. Therefore, as will be detailed below, a crisis in the economy points to a serious problem in society—namely in human relations.

WHAT IS A CRISIS?

> Merriam-Webster's Dictionary defines a crisis as "The turning point for better or worse." Also, "The decisive moment," and "An unstable or crucial time or state of affairs in which a decisive change is impending," or "A situation that has reached a critical phase."
>
> In Greek, *krisis,* literally means, "decision," from *krinein,* "to decide."

The connection among people throughout the world has grown much closer in the last few decades. Globalization has created a flow of goods, services, information, and people from place to place, effectively "shrinking" the world into a global village. Ian Goldin, Director of Oxford Martin School at the University of Oxford, and former Vice President of the World Bank stated in a lecture: "Globalization is getting more complex, and this change is getting more rapid. The future will be more unpredictable. ...What happens in one place very quickly affects everything else. This is a systemic risk."[15]

Globalization has made it clear that we are all connected to and dependent on one another like cogwheels in a machine. An event that occurs in one area of the planet can instigate a domino effect that sends ripples throughout the world.

The trade connections in the car industry between the U.S. and Japan exemplify how interdependence is the name of the game in a globalized world. The devastating earthquake and tsunami that struck Japan on March 11, 2011 hampered the chain of production and import of cars and car parts from Japan to the U.S. Although it adversely affected the production lines of Japanese carmakers' factories in the U.S., it positively affected other car makers, who gained market share because of Japan's troubles.

The financial market is perhaps the best example of international interdependence. Government bonds bought by other governments keep economies and indeed countries locked in unbreakable ties. The Chinese government, for example, must buy U.S. bonds so that Americans can buy Chinese goods, thus maintaining China's rapid growth and preventing it from suffering from unemployment.

Editor of Newsweek International, Fareed Zakaria, eloquently described this entanglement in a *Newsweek* article titled, "Get Out the Wallets: The world needs Americans to spend": "If I were told by the economic gods that I could have the answer to one question about the fate of the global economy... I would ask, 'When will the American consumer start spending again?'"[16] Indeed, we have become a global village, completely reliant on one another for our sustenance.

A more recent example of global interdependence is the American debt ceiling crisis. In July of 2011, the U.S.

needed to set a new debt ceiling. However, the political struggle between Republicans and Democrats caused them to nearly miss the deadline for setting the ceiling. The world was afraid that America would stop buying because it had exceeded its debt ceiling. Consequently, stock markets around the world plummeted. Although no one really expects America to repay its colossal debt, which now exceeds 100% of its GDP,[17] and passed the 15 trillion dollar mark,[18] everyone still waited anxiously for America to sort out its political dispute so the world could keep working. After all, if America were to default on its debt, tens of millions of workers worldwide would be out of work within days.

> Prof. Tim Jackson, economics commissioner on the UK government's Sustainable Development Commission, said about globalization: "It's a story about us, people, being persuaded to spend money we don't have on things we don't need, to create impressions that won't last, on people we don't care about."[19]

The Eurozone crisis, where Germany and France are having to pay for the bailouts and rescue programs of the PIIGS countries (Portugal, Ireland, Italy, Greece, and Spain), is another example of economic interdependence. While it may seem unfair that German citizens have to pay for Greece's past squandering, in truth, much of what the Greeks were spending their money on was German goods, which kept German workers employed and paying taxes. So there is a two-way bargain here, with the Greeks helping Germany maintain its economic strength in return for Germany bailing the Greeks out when they are broke. Interdependence at work!

In the past, the world was an aggregate of isolated parts, but as the network of global connections grew stronger, we found ourselves in a new, volatile, unpredictable world. Renowned sociologist Anthony Giddens expressed that bewilderment succinctly yet accurately: "For better or worse, we are being propelled into a global order that no one fully understands, but which is making its effects felt upon all of us."[20]

Without planning it, we have moved from independently rowing our personal boats in the sea of life into being all in the same boat, as Christine Lagarde pointed out in her above-quoted address. And because now we are all in the same boat, clearly we are all dependent on one another. This means that unless we all agree on the direction in which we wish to sail, we will not be able to advance in any direction whatsoever, as demonstrated by the global slowdown. Imagine what happens when myriad people turn in myriad directions all at the same time. The obvious result is that we are stuck in paralysis, which is the current state of the world.

To better understand that paralysis, think of a married couple having a marriage breakdown. When the crisis peaks, they are so resentful of each other that they cannot tolerate living side by side. While they are still living in the same house, they can't wait for the moment when they part ways. In such a tense state, the walls seem to be pressing them together, but at the same time, their repulsion presses them away from each other. Like that married couple, we are hateful towards each other. But unlike the couple, we cannot leave because there is no other Earth for us to inhabit.

> "Because interdependence exposes everyone around the world in an unprecedented way, governing global risks is humanity's great challenge. Think of climate change; the risks of nuclear energy...; terrorist threats...; the collateral effects of political instability; the economic repercussions of financial crises; epidemics...; and sudden, media-fueled panics, such as Europe's recent cucumber crisis. All of these phenomena form a part of the dark side of the globalized world: contamination, contagion, instability, interconnection, turbulence, shared fragility... Interdependency is, in fact, mutual dependency—a shared exposure to hazards. Nothing is completely isolated, and 'foreign affairs' no longer exists... Other people's problems are now our problems, and we can no longer look on them with indifference, or hope to reap some personal gain from them."
>
> Javier Solana, former Secretary General of NATO[21]

To cope with the modern reality, we must be considerate of the global, connected nature of the world that appears before us. And here is where science comes to our aid. Connected systems are nothing new; the whole of Nature consists of such systems. The human body—a comparison that will be used frequently in this book—is a great example of a connected system. All the organs in the body are connected and work in synchrony and reciprocity. Each cell and organ in the body "knows" its role and performs it, thus benefiting the entire organism: the heart pumps blood to the rest of the body, the lungs absorb oxygen for the rest of the body, and the liver filters the blood for the rest of the body.

At the same time, each organ in our body is also a consumer, receiving from the body all it needs for its sustenance. And yet, the purpose of existence of each organ is not self-centered, meaning the benefit of the organ, but organism-centered, meaning the benefit of the *entire* organism. Organs exist as parts of a collective that together form a single, complete unit. Without the context of that unit, we would not be able to fully understand the function or purpose of each organ. The nutrients that each organ receives from the body enable it to function and realize the purpose of its existence, its unique role with respect to the rest of the organism, and realize its full potential by "sharing" its product with the entire organism. This is the prime condition of life in a community.

When one of the systems in the organism does not perform its function, the organism deteriorates into a state called "illness." If the state of illness is prolonged or acute, it could lead to the collapse of the entire system and the death of the organism.

The global human society and the changes that have occurred in the world over the last few decades indicate that humanity is becoming an integrated, interconnected system, like the rest of the systems in Nature. Therefore, the laws that define the mutual connections among elements in Nature now apply to the human society, as well.

> "The 21st century, unlike the period after the Congress of Vienna, is no longer a zero-sum game of winners and losers. Rather, it is a century of multiple networked nodes. The better these nodes are connected with each other, the more they will resonate with the best ideals and principles."
> **Professor Dr. Ludger Kunhardt,**
> **Director at the Center for European Integration Studies[22]**

Until recently, we felt that each of us was a more or less an independent unit. We built a society that allowed everyone to succeed on its own, even when that success often came at the expense of others.

But the network of connections that is now developing tells us that this approach can no longer work. The old way has exhausted itself, and now it has been upgraded. To continue to advance, we must work with the new functionality that has taken over in accord with globalization. And to do that, we must connect to one another and work together.

There are already numerous experts in many fields who explain that the old world is falling apart right before our eyes because it is based on a self-centered approach whose time has gone. The new world requires us to reconstruct all systems and processes based on a new approach of collaboration and mutual guarantee, where all are guarantors of each other's well-being. In the coming years, we will all have to learn how to work together to ensure our survival. Each person, each society, each nation, and each state will have to learn to work together.

> "The real challenge today is to change our way of thinking—not just our systems, institutions or policies. We need the imagination to grasp the immense promise—and challenge—of the interconnected world we have created. ...The future lies with more globalization, not less, more cooperation, more interaction between peoples and cultures, and even greater sharing of responsibilities and interests. It is unity in our global diversity that we need today."
>
> Pascal Lamy, Director-General of the
> World Trade Organization (WTO)[23]

The solution to our present crisis depends first and foremost on changing ourselves and adjusting to the new reality. For this reason, throughout the world people are beginning to change their behavior—they are beginning to sense that their governments are not functioning properly and cannot provide solutions to their problems. Many feel a need to go out to the street and congregate with others of like mind.

They mention many reasons for such gatherings, depending on the country. In the Arab world they are protesting for democracy and freedom of speech. In Europe they are demanding solutions to the problems of unemployment and austerity measures, and in America it is the 1% who are wealthy vs. the 99% who are not.

Once people come together in protest, they are aware of a new sense of empowerment. You can sense it in tent cities throughout Europe, in the "Occupy Movement" in the U.S., and even in Egypt, where people continually take to the streets because they feel that together they have the power to get what they want. Even when they cannot quite verbalize *what* it is they want, such as in the early days of the Occupy Movement, it is clear that people enjoy the experience of a genuine democracy where all decisions are made in a group spirit, rather than through lobbying and political maneuverings.

The togetherness of the protesters aligns with the new laws of the globalized world. This congruence adds power to the protests, power to which governments cannot remain indifferent. However, for the protests to succeed, they must remain in harmony with the law of globalization. Any solution that favors one sector or faction over another is just as self-centered as the current system, and therefore bound to fail.

Today, any pressure group that benefits only itself at the expense of others will only intensify the power struggles that already exist, and will accelerate the decline of the society and the economy of that country. The new state of the world necessitates that all of us, from ordinary citizens to decision-makers, resolve our problems through deliberation, consideration, and mutual guarantee.

"Our well-being is inextricably intertwined with
that of strangers from around the globe. ...At
some point, we'll have to move beyond fighting
mode and adapt to our interconnectedness. As
Clinton put it, 'We find as our interdependence
increases ... we do better when other people do
better as well, so we have to find ways that we can
all win.'"

Gregory Rodriguez, founding director of the Center
for Social Cohesion at Arizona State University[24]

The new world requires that we revolutionize our
relations, not by force, but in our hearts. It must happen
within each and every one of us. In Chapters 3 and 4, we
will discuss the means at our disposal to succeed with this
revolution. For now, let's just say that the purpose of this
revolution in our perception is to expand our awareness
from "me" to "we," to pull us out of our narrow cubes
into our great, common sphere.

There is no doubt that we are living in a special time.
The mutual guarantee among us presents itself as the law
of life in our connected world. In the next chapter, we
will see that not only are all humans connected, but that
we and the whole of Nature form a single unit.

"I asked the Dalai Lama what is the key to Peace?
He said, 'Think We, not Me or I.'"

Kenro Izu, founder of Friends without a Border[25]

Nature and Us

"A human being is part of the whole called by
us 'universe.' ...We experience ourselves, our
thoughts, and feelings as something separate
from the rest, a kind of optical delusion of
consciousness."

Albert Einstein, in a letter dated 1950[26]

L et's take a short break from the hustle and bustle
of life in the postmodern, self-entitlement-inflicted
age and see where the concept of mutual guarantee
comes from. Deep in the heart of the vast universe lies a
spiral galaxy of no particular distinction. Within it is an
average-looking star with planets and asteroids surrounding
it, like numerous other stars in the universe.

But on the third-removed planet from the star there
is a phenomenon that doesn't exist on the other planets,

perhaps on none but that one planet, although the universe is too big to know for certain. That phenomenon is called "life."

Life is a peculiar phenomenon in that it is dynamic and constantly changing. However, it does not change randomly, but rather in a very clear direction—from simplex to complex, from separation to integration. Right after the Big Bang, "The universe was dominated by radiation," explains a publication by the MIT Haystack Observatory.[27] "Soon, quarks combined together to form baryons (protons and neutrons). When the universe was three minutes old, it had cooled enough for these protons and neutrons to combine into nuclei."

The process of growing integration and complexity continued, forming galaxies, stars, and planets. On at least one of those planets, the process continued beyond the mineral level and into the organic level, otherwise known as "life." This was made possible when organic materials combined in a way that gave them a unique quality—self-replication. As they continued to merge in sync with the course of evolution, they grew even more sophisticated, learning specialized tasks and benefiting the entire congregation of cells (or molecules within a cell). They relied on the rest of the elements in the group to provide for their necessities while they continued providing their unique functions for the others. These were Nature's first examples of mutual guarantee, and the principles that applied to those cell colonies billions of years ago still apply today to every living thing.

After approximately four billion years, the human race appeared on earth. Humans, unlike the rest of Nature, feel that they are distinct, separate from other aspects of Nature. We feel that we are superior, not part of an entire system but above it. The trait that humanity has indeed introduced into Nature's system is the sense of self-entitlement. All other animals, plants, and minerals perform their tasks as Nature dictates, through instincts and acquired behaviors. We, on the other hand, have the freedom of choice to work for our own interests, or for those of others in our society.

If we look at Nature, we will see that in truth, choosing mutual guarantee and preferring the interests of society over self-interests are more beneficial to the individual. As we explained in regard to the body in the previous chapter, no organism could exist if its cells operated only for themselves. Likewise, no human could exist if we all had to work for ourselves. Imagine the seven billion people on earth farming the land only for themselves, digging wells and pumping waters only for themselves, and hunting for food and clothing only for themselves. What would happen to our society? Indeed, what would happen to *us*?

Thus, it is self-interest that makes us work together, but there is something within us that urges us to work for ourselves, seemingly overlooking our actual interdependence. Returning to the example of the human body, evolutionary biologist Elisabet Sahtouris eloquently explained the concept of interdependence among self-centered elements in a presentation she gave at a conference in Tokyo in November 2005: "In your body, every molecule, every cell, every organ ... has self-interest. When every level... shows its self-interest, it forces negotiations among the levels. This is the secret of Nature. Every moment in your body, these negotiations drive your system to harmony."

If we could see that evolution continues today and did not stop when homo sapiens appeared, we would realize that the direction from simplex to complex, from separation to integration continues to be Nature's course. The only difference from times before is that the human species is not forced to integrate, but must choose integration over separation. If it does, a life of harmony, balance, and prosperity will ensue.

It follows that the process by which the world has become a global village is not a unique incident, but a natural extension of the nearly 14 billion years of evolution since the Big Bang. The crisis that humanity is experiencing today is not the collapse of civilization, but the emergence of a new stage in which humanity, too, becomes a single entity, conscious of its interconnectedness and working in harmony with it. When we achieve that awareness, we will be as a single organism, within which every organ works to benefit the whole, while the rest of the organism provides for the organ's every need.

COMPLEMENTARITY AND RECIPROCITY

"Unity and complementarity constitute reality,"[28]
Werner Heisenberg, physicist, formulated the Uncertainty Principle

A deeper examination of Nature unveils the profound bond that sustains it. Each element complements other elements and serves them, as demonstrated by the food chain: Plants feed on minerals, herbivores feed on plants, and carnivores feed on herbivores. This chain contains myriad sub-chains that together form the entire food chain. In the food chain, every element affects every other element, and any change in one of them will affect every other element in the chain.

Studying Nature reveals that each element that performs its function allows ecosystems to maintain balance among the different elements in the system, thus keeping it healthy. An eye-opening report submitted to the U.S. Department of Education in October, 2003 by Irene Sanders and Judith McCabe, PhD, clearly demonstrates what happens when we breach Nature's balance. "In 1991, an orca—a killer whale—was seen eating a sea otter. Orcas and otters usually coexist peacefully. So, what happened? Ecologists found that ocean perch and herring were also declining. Orcas don't eat those fish, but seals and sea lions do. And seals and sea lions are what orcas usually eat, and their population had also declined. So deprived of their seals and sea lions, orcas started turning to the playful sea otters for dinner.

"So otters have vanished because the fish, which they never ate in the first place, have vanished. Now, the ripple spreads. Otters are no longer there to eat sea urchins, so the sea urchin population has exploded. But sea urchins live off seafloor kelp forests, so they're killing off the kelp. Kelp has been home to fish that feed seagulls and eagles. Like orcas, seagulls can find other food, but bald eagles can't and they're in trouble.

"All this began with the decline of ocean perch and herring. Why? Well, Japanese whalers have been killing off the variety of whales that eat the same microscopic organisms that feed pollock [a type of carnivorous fish]. With more fish to eat, pollock flourish. They in turn attack the perch and herring that were food for the seals and sea lions. With the decline in the population of sea lions and seals, the orcas must turn to otters."

NATURE AND ECOLOGY

As we have seen, Nature consists of reciprocal connections that create balance, congruence, and harmony. But humans do not operate in this reciprocal manner, neither among themselves nor between themselves and Nature. Therefore, since humans are a part of Nature, their lack of congruence with it and among themselves throws the entire system off balance, as the previous example of the orcas demonstrated. While the whole of Nature follows the principle of mutual guarantee—give what you can and receive what you need—humans operate to the contrary— take what you can and give what you must. We humans exploit one another, and all of us as humanity exploit Nature. Indeed, we have nearly depleted our planet of its resources.

> "Our ecological footprints are already using the renewable resources of 1.4 planet Earths, and probably will be using that of two planet Earths by 2050. In other words, we are living unsustainably and depleting the earth's natural capital. No one knows how long we can continue on this path, but environmental alarm bells are going off."
>
> G. Tyler Miller, Scott Spoolman,
> Living in the Environment: Principles, Connections, and Solutions[29]

Human beings have become a cancer-like tumor in Nature. Humanity is sucking up everything for itself, irrespective of the environment. But just as cancer dies along with the organism that it puts to death, so, too, will humanity if it does not transform itself into a healthy organ in the organism of Nature.

To understand why humanity is behaving in this irresponsible, irrational manner, we need to take a closer look at human nature. As biologist Sahtouris explained in the above-mentioned quote, "Every molecule, every cell, every organ ... has self-interest." Yet, self-interest does not mean that humankind must be oblivious to the fact that maintaining the well-being of the organism—which is humanity—is in one's self-interest.

What obscures that fact from us is our sense of *entitlement*, or "narcissism." Psychologists Jean M. Twenge and Keith Campbell describe our society as "increasingly narcissistic."[30] In their insightful book, *The Narcissism Epidemic: Living in the Age of Entitlement*, Twenge and Campbell talk about "The relentless rise of narcissism in our culture,"[31] and the problems it causes. "The United States is currently suffering from an epidemic of narcissism. ...narcissistic personality traits rose just as fast as obesity," they explain. "Worse yet," they continue, "the rise in narcissism is accelerating, with scores rising faster in the 2000s than in previous decades. By 2006, 1 out of 4 college students agreed with the majority of the items on a standard measure of narcissistic traits. Today, as singer Little Jackie put it, many people feel that 'Yes, siree, the whole world should revolve around me.'"[32]

In Webster's Dictionary, narcissism is defined as "egoism," and this, to be blunt, means that we have become unbearably selfish.

Our overblown egoism has led us to develop a culture of consumerism, which entails the aggressive production, marketing, and consumption of goods and services not because they genuinely improve our lives, but because we can show them off. We buy because others buy, because we don't want to be left behind.

Consumerism has caused every industry to accelerate its production, resulting in a slew of redundancies produced at an alarming rate. These are now polluting the planet and depleting it of its resources only to cater to the never-ending pursuit of wealth and social status. But there is a limit to everything, and we have nearly reached the end of our rope.

Following the 2011 International Energy Agency (IEA) report, *Internatonal Energy Outlook 2011*, Fatih Birol, chief economist at the agency told Fiona Harvey of *The Guardian*, "The door is closing. I am very worried--if we don't change direction now on how we use energy, we will end up beyond what scientists tell us is the minimum [for safety]. The door will be closed forever."[33]

Similarly, a digest by Yale University reports, "A draft report by the Intergovernmental Panel on Climate Change (IPCC) says there is a 2-in-3 probability that human-caused climate change is already leading to an increase in extreme weather events. The draft summary ... said that increasingly wild weather ... will lead to a growing toll in lost lives and property damage, and will render some locations 'increasingly marginal as places to live.' The report says that scientists are 'virtually certain' that continued warming will cause not only an increase in extreme heat waves and drought in some regions, but also will generate more intense downpours that lead to severe flooding."[34]

Humankind's lack of concern for the environment has already been disastrous to our most vital needs— our sources of food and water. Already, according to the World Wildlife Fund (WWF), "Over fishing ... is devastating fish populations. Over 75 percent of fisheries are already fully exploited or over fished."[35]

Also, Ian Sample of *The Guardian* writes, "Some 40% of the world's agricultural land is seriously degraded. The UN millennium ecosystem assessment ranked land degradation among the world's greatest environmental challenges, claiming it risked destabilizing societies, endangering food security, and increasing poverty."[36]

But the facts about water—the most essential substance for all life—are the most alarming. An official publication by the United Nations Children's Fund (UNICEF) details the harm and danger of drinking unsafe water: "Almost fifty per cent of the developing world's population—2.5 billion people—lack improved sanitation facilities, and over 884 million people still use unsafe drinking water sources. Inadequate access to safe water and sanitation services, coupled with poor hygiene practices, kills and sickens thousands of children every day, and leads to impoverishment and diminished opportunities for thousands more. Poor sanitation, water, and hygiene have many other serious repercussions. Children—and particularly girls—are denied their right to education because their schools lack ... decent sanitation facilities. Women are forced to spend large parts of their day fetching water. Poor farmers and wage earners are less productive due to illness, health systems are overwhelmed, and national economies suffer. Without WASH (water, sanitation and hygiene), sustainable development is impossible."[37]

> "Since it is the destruction of the economy's natural supports and disruption of the climate system that are driving the world toward the edge, these are the trends that must be reversed. To do so requires extraordinarily demanding measures, a fast shift away from business as usual."

"As land and water become scarce, as the earth's temperature rises, and as world food security deteriorates, a dangerous geopolitics of food scarcity is emerging."

Lester R. Brown, environmental analyst, founder and president of the Earth Policy Institute, and author of *World on the Edge: How to Prevent Environmental and Economic Collapse*[38]

On May 6, 2011, Matthew Lee of the *Associated Press*, reported, "U.S. Secretary of State, Hillary Rodham Clinton, warned that global shortages of food and spiraling prices threaten widespread destabilization and is urging immediate action to forestall a repeat of the 2007 and 2008 crisis that led to riots in dozens of countries around the developing world. ...The U.N. estimates that 44 million people have been pushed into poverty since last June because of rising food prices, which could lead to desperate shortages and unrest. Clinton said the world could no longer 'keep falling back on providing emergency aid to keep the Band-Aid on.'"[39]

Sadly, a week later came the disheartening report that "The world wastes 30% of all food."[40] According to the report, "30% of all food produced in the world each year is wasted or lost. That's about 1.3 billion tons, according to a new report by the U.N. Food and Agriculture Organization. ...That's as if each person in China, the world's most populous country with more than 1.3 billion people, had a one ton mass of food they could just throw into the trash can. ...Breaking apart that big number, we find the people with the most money are the ones who waste the most. ...And these numbers come as we've just been reporting about soaring food prices around the world in the past week." "A major change of mindset is what is needed," concluded CNN reporter Ramy Inocencio.

Indeed, we need to shift our mindset into one supporting mutual guarantee. With such a mindset, no food will be thrown into the trash when there are people in the world who go to bed hungry. In a mutual guarantee society, this would be tantamount to letting your own family starve while gorging yourself to obesity.

Michel Camdessus, former Managing Director of the International Monetary Fund (IMF) for 13 years, explains the connection between the state of the economy, the state of the environment, and the lack of mutual guarantee, which he sees as the origin of both crises. "What has taken place is a kind of ethical, global problem. For years and years, we have allowed all the sound warnings ... to the financial actors to moderate their financial appetites, to care about the community, to care about their neighbors—all these principles have been forgotten. We must reestablish a kind of global, ethical system, which is missing. ...Both of them [financial and environmental crisis] find their origins in the over-exploitation of the natural resources or of the economic mechanisms. All of that means that all of us must rethink our own conception models; we must all be more conscious that in the years to come we'll have more responsibilities."[41]

Yet, despite the obvious limits on Earth's resources and the growing evidence of the damage we have caused, we keep "milking" Mother Earth, needlessly polluting the air, water, and ground, leaving a planet for our children that will provide them with neither food nor energy.

Concerning our continuing depletion of these limited energy sources, Steve Connor of *The Independent* interviewed Fatih Birol, chief economist of the IEA. According to Connor, "Dr. Birol said that the public and many governments appeared to be oblivious to the fact that the oil on which modern civilization depends is running out far faster than previously predicted and that global production is likely to peak in about 10 years— at least a decade earlier than most governments had estimated."[42]

RESTORING THE BALANCE

"Till now, man has been up against Nature; from now on, he will be up against his own nature."[43]

Dennis Gabor, inventor of holography,
winner of the 1971 Nobel Prize in Physics

Balance is the name of the game in Nature. It is the state to which Nature aspires to bring all its elements. The only reason why any substance or object moves or changes is its "aspiration" to restore balance. That aspiration creates such phenomena as wind, spreading of heat into cooler areas, the flow of water toward lower grounds, and many other phenomena. In living organisms, a state of balance is called "homeostasis" (from Greek, *hómoios*, "similar" and *stásis*, "standing still"). Webster's dictionary defines homeostasis as "A relatively stable state of equilibrium or a tendency toward such a state between the different but interdependent elements or groups of elements of an organism, population, or group."

We, as different but interdependent parts of Nature, are subject to the law of balance, or "homeostasis," in our bodies, as well as in our entire population, as defined by Webster's. That is, humanity is not a distinct entity, but an integrated part of Nature. For this reason, we are subject to all of Nature's laws in our bodies and in our societies.

On the human level, "being in homeostasis" means expanding our awareness from self-centeredness to social-centeredness and even global-centeredness. We need to increase our consideration of others and our environment, all of which are parts of the system that includes us. The examples presented above illustrate some of the consequences we may suffer if we choose to remain oblivious to our interconnectedness with each other and with Nature.

LABOR PANGS

"We are challenged to rise above the narrow confines of our individualistic concerns to the broader concerns of all humanity. The new world is a world of geographical togetherness. This means that no individual or nation can live alone. We must all learn to live together, or we will be forced to die together."

Martin Luther King, Jr.[44]

Now that human egoism is posing a threat to our existence, we are faced with two choices. We can sit idly, let Nature take its course, and wait for troubles to knock on our door before we contemplate how to address them. Or, we can take action and assume responsibility for our future. Today the human race can still advance toward balance and harmony with Nature, and toward sustainable prosperity. All we need is to implement the approach of mutual guarantee, thus becoming synchronized with Nature.

By doing so, the society that we will build will be sustainable, prosperous, secure, and peaceful–since there can hardly be war amongst those who vouch for each other's well-being.

The next chapter will discuss the practical steps we can take to establish such a civilization.

The Practical Way

"The great project of the twenty-first century—
understanding how the whole of humanity comes
to be greater than the sum of its parts—is just
beginning. Like an awakening child, the human
superorganism is becoming self-aware, and this
will surely help us achieve our goals."

N. Christakis & J. Fowler, *Connected: The Surprising Power of Our
Social Networks*[45]

In the previous chapters we described the connections that link the entire world into a single network. We realized that this network is a natural creation of evolution, which moves from simplex to complex, from separation to integration. This connectedness also determines that mutual guarantee is the formula by which all life sustains itself, and that if humanity wishes to be sustainable, we need to apply that *modus operandi* to ourselves.

The only issue that remains is how we should do this. Indeed, how does an individual, or a society, shift from a mindset of caring for oneself into caring for all? Put differently, "How do we shift from the 'me' mode to the 'we' mode?" Moreover, that transformation must not be random, but become a lasting shift from the self-centered trend that Twenge and Campbell described in the previously quoted, *The Narcissism Epidemic*.

The way we can achieve this is by changing our social values. If we look deep into the reasons for our behavior, we will discover that quite often we act certain ways to gain social approval from those around us. Being appreciated by those in our social environment gives us confidence and high spirits, while the lack of it pains us, making us insecure and ashamed of who we are. For this reason, consciously or not, we tend to conform to society's codes of behavior and values.

Maria Konnikova, the eloquent writer and psychologist, wrote about our need to conform to society's codes in her blog on *Scientific American*: "We tend to behave quite differently when we expect to be observed than when we don't and we are acutely responsive to prevailing social mores and social norms. ...When we decide to do something, should it matter to us whether or not someone else is watching? While theoretically, it's easy to argue that it shouldn't, that the same behavioral norms apply no matter what, in practice, it usually does. This goes for minor behaviors (Will you pick your nose in public? What about if you're pretty sure no one is watching you?) as well as much more important ones (Will you hurt someone, be it physically or otherwise, if others are observing your interaction? What about if you're fairly certain the misdeed will never go beyond the two of you?)."[46]

Therefore, as soon as we change our society's values so that mutual guarantee and caring for each other are at the top tier, we will change our values accordingly. When society values people according to their contribution to society, people will also wish to contribute to society, so they, too, can be appreciated. If respect and social statuses that are currently given for excellence in financial engineering—whose consequences we are still grappling with—were given to individuals who improved the overall well-being of society, whether financially or in other forms of value, then everyone would begin to contribute to society in that constructive manner.

CHANGING THE PUBLIC DISCOURSE

The impact of public opinion had been powerfully demonstrated during much of 2011 via the global unrest unleashed first in the Arab world and Europe, and then worldwide, fueled by social media, and then official and traditional media. If you look up the concept of the 1% vs. the 99%, you will find almost no mention of it before the Occupy Wall Street (OWS) movement began its protests on September 17, 2011.

Another acknowledgment of the power of social discourse and public opinion to improve society came in a written statement by the World Bank titled, "The Power of Public Discourse": "The concept of open development [granting equal trade opportunities to all] presupposes a greatly increased supply of information available to citizens. ...The purpose of all this [open development] is to create a shift in the power relationship from the institutions and governments, whose responsibility it is to provide services and improve lives, to the people whom those services are supposed to benefit. That power can be effectively exercised by small groups of citizens working together to identify and confront politicians or service providers who are failing to deliver the services for which money is available. Because corruption and political or self-interest are heavily entrenched, more open development is unlikely to have the desired effects unless various publics are able, collectively and peacefully, to exert public influence."[47]

The effectiveness of the influence of the environment was scientifically proven decades ago. In 1951, one of the most renowned studies on the subject was conducted by psychologist Solomon Eliot Asch. That study became known as the Asch Conformity Experiment. Using the Line Judgment Task, Asch put a naive participant in a room with seven confederates. The confederates had agreed in advance what their responses would be when presented with the line task. The real participant did not know this and was led to believe that the other seven participants were also real participants.

Each person in the room had to state aloud which comparison line (A, B, or C) was most like the target line. The answer was always obvious. The real participant sat at the end of the row and gave his or her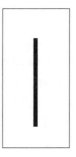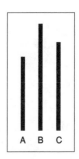
answer last. There were 18 trials in total and the bogus participants gave the wrong answer on 12 trails.

Results: On average, about one third (32%) of the participants who were placed in this situation went along and conformed with the clearly incorrect majority. Over the 18 trials about 75% of participants conformed at least once and 25% of the participants never conformed.

Conclusion: Why did the participants conform so readily? When they were interviewed after the experiment, most of them said that they did not really believe their conforming answers, but had gone along with the group for fear of being ridiculed or thought peculiar. A few of them said that they really did believe the group's answers were correct.

Apparently, people conform for two main reasons: because they want to fit in with the group (normative influence) and because they believe the group is better informed than they are (informational influence).[48]

A new study proves the rather Orwellian notion that the influence of one's social environment can even change one's memories. A study at the Weizmann Institute of

Science tested to what extent people's memories could be altered through social manipulation. The release by the Weizmann Institute declared, "New research at the Weizmann Institute shows that a bit of social pressure may be all that is needed." The experiment took place in four stages. First, volunteers watched a film. Three days later, they took a memory test, answering questions about the film. They were also asked how confident they were about their answers.

They were later invited to retake the test while being scanned in a functional magnetic resonance imager (fMRI) that revealed their brain activity. This time, the subjects were also given the supposed answers of the others in their viewing group. Planted among these were false answers to questions the volunteers had previously answered correctly and confidently. After seeing these "planted" responses, the participants conformed to the group, giving incorrect answers nearly 70% of the time.

But were they simply conforming to social demands, or had their memory of the film actually changed? To find out, the researchers invited the subjects to retake the memory test. In some cases the respondents reverted back to the original, correct ones; however, close to half remained erroneous, implying that the subjects were relying on false memories implanted in the earlier session.

An analysis of the fMRI data showed differences in brain activity between the persistent false memories and the temporary errors of social compliance. The scientists think there is a link connecting the social and the memory processing parts of the brain: "Its 'stamp' may be needed ... to give [memories] approval before they get uploaded to the memory bank. Thus, social reinforcement could act on ... our brains to replace a strong memory with a false one." [49]

> "Most people are not even aware of their need to conform. They live under the illusion that they follow their own ideas and inclinations, that they are individualists, that they have arrived at their opinions as the result of their own thinking - and that it just happens that their ideas are the same as the majority."
>
> Erich Fromm, *The Art of Loving*[50]

Now that we have seen how society affects people's views, let's examine the issue from a practical, educational angle. The impact of the media on our views, even physically on our brains, has been documented and recognized more than once. Headlines such as "Violent Video Games and Changes in the Brain,"[51] "Norwegian Retailer Pulls Violent Games In Wake of Attack,"[52] and "Mass Shooting in Germany Prompts Retailer to Drop Mature-Rated Games"[53] indicate that people are well aware of the harm of violent and aggressive media. Yet, for all our awareness, the media not only keeps showing these offending images, but even increases their frequency and explicitness.

To understand how much violence young minds absorb, consider this piece of information from a

University of Michigan Health System publication titled, "Television and Children": "An average American child will see 200,000 violent acts and 16,000 murders on TV by age 18."[54] If this number doesn't seem alarming, consider that there are 6,570 days in eighteen years, which means that on average, by age eighteen a child will have watched slightly more than thirty acts of violence on TV, 2.4 of which are murders, *every day of his or her young life.*

> "It is not neutrality for which we are demanded, but rather unity, unity of common guarantee, of mutual responsibility, of reciprocity... This is where our work in education among our youngsters aims, and even more so with the adults."
>
> Martin Buber, philosopher and educator,
> *A Nation and a World: Essays on current events*[55]

To conclude, contemporary research proves that "my environment today is me tomorrow." Our environments build us as human beings, and because we are products of our environments, every change that we wish to impose on ourselves must first be absorbed into our environments. Therefore, when we build an environment in which the value of mutual guarantee is endorsed and is deemed praiseworthy, that value will be praiseworthy in our own eyes, as well.

IMPLEMENTATION: INTERNET AND INTERPERSONAL COMMUNICATION

The quickest and most obvious solution to achieving the shift in our values is through the key elements that design our thought patterns today—the media and the internet. To change the social mindset, we need to change the discourse in the media. As we demonstrated above, if the media were to tell us that giving, sharing, and collaborating were good, we would think so, too, and would gladly follow suit.

But in today's reality, our egos are boosted, self-entitlement is rewarded, and manipulative people are given the positive moniker of "Go-getter." It is hardly surprising that those who are not selfish and mean at school tend to be labeled as "dorks" or "weak." It is also not surprising that with such an influx of socially negative messages, police officers must be placed in every elementary school in Texas, for example, not to keep dangerous adults away, but to keep dangerous *children* away, and even arrest some of them at age 6! And not just one or two, but 300,000 children in 2010 alone, and just in that one state.[56]

Entertaining TV does not have to mean violent or self-entitlement-promoting shows. It is quite possible to produce entertaining, high-quality TV that contains prosocial messages. Investigative journalism can expose not only corruption, but also show how we all depend on each other, and how only together we can succeed. The media can introduce communities and initiatives where such concepts are being implemented, such as the town of Marinaleda in Spain, as presented in *The New York Times'* inspiring story, "A Job and No Mortgage for All in a Spanish Town."[57]

The media can then discuss to what extent such efforts are successful, to what extent and how they improve our lives, and how applicable such initiatives are in different parts of the world.

The bottom line is that the public discourse needs to change, and when it does people will change their views and the media will change its content to suit the public discourse. But the change must begin with a conscious effort, as the current trend of the media is anti-social rather than prosocial.

Also, today a social change doesn't have to begin at the top, on a prime time, high-profile TV show on the most popular channels. It can just as successfully be a grassroots movement with a few enthusiasts who join to form a social movement that will be promoted through the internet. This is precisely how the OWS movement began.

Social media outlets such as Facebook and YouTube allow anyone with just a little bit of drive and gumption to promote any idea they wish—good or bad—and create enough buzz around it to gather a critical mass of prosocial ideas. As we will see below, it takes a small, determined minority to make a quick, big, and decisive change.

Alongside the various media outlets, there is the good old word-of-mouth circulation. Ideas spread best by simply talking about them—at home, at work, with friends, on online forums, and through social networks. Simply telling people what you believe is right will get them thinking.

"Nothing beats coming up with a product so interesting that people just can't help talking about it. Nothing is better than customers taking it upon themselves to support a business that they just love," writes marketing consultant, Andy Sernovitz, in his book, *Word of Mouth Marketing: How Smart Companies Get People Talking, Revised Edition*.[58]

There is even a more latent side to the spreading of ideas. They can spread far and wide by people simply thinking about or wanting certain things. On September 10, 2009, *The New York Times* published a story titled, "Are Your Friends Making You Fat?" by Clive Thompson.[59] In his story, Thompson describes a fascinating experiment performed in Framingham, Massachusetts. In the experiment, details of the lives of 15,000 people were documented and registered periodically over fifty years. Professors Nicholas Christakis' and James Fowler's analysis of the data revealed astonishing discoveries about how we affect one another on all levels—physical, emotional, and mental—and how ideas can be as contagious as viruses.

In their celebrated book, *Connected: The Surprising Power of Our Social Networks and How They Shape Our Lives—How Your Friends' Friends' Friends Affect Everything You Feel, Think, and Do*, Christakis and Fowler established that there was a network of interrelations among more than 5,000 of the participants. Christakis and Fowler discovered that in the network, people affected each other and were affected by each other not just in social issues, but with physical issues, as well.

"By analyzing the Framingham data," Thompson wrote, "Christakis and Fowler say they have for the first time found some solid basis for a potentially powerful theory in epidemiology: that good behaviors—like quitting smoking or staying slender or being happy— pass from friend to friend almost as if they were contagious viruses. The Framingham participants, the data suggested, influenced one another's health just by socializing. And the same was true of bad behaviors— clusters of friends appeared to 'infect' each other with obesity, unhappiness, and smoking. Staying healthy isn't just a matter of your genes and your diet, it seems. Good health is also a product, in part, of your sheer proximity to other healthy people."[60]

Even more surprising was the researchers' discovery that these infections could "jump" across connections. They discovered that people can affect each other even if they do not know each other! Moreover, Christakis and Fowler found evidence of these effects even three degrees apart (friend of a friend of a friend). In Thompson's words, "When a Framingham resident became obese, his or her friends were 57 percent more likely to become obese, too. Even more astonishing... it appeared to skip links. A Framingham resident was roughly 20 percent more likely to become obese if the friend of a friend became obese—even if the connecting friend didn't put on a single pound. Indeed, a person's risk of obesity went up about 10 percent even if a friend of a friend of a friend gained weight."[61]

Quoting Professor Christakis, Thompson wrote, "In some sense we can begin to understand human emotions like happiness the way we might study the stampeding of buffalo. You don't ask an individual buffalo, 'Why are you running to the left?' The answer is that the whole herd is running to the left."[62]

But there is more to social contagion than watching one's weight or heart condition. In a televised lecture, Professor Christakis explained that our social lives (and hence much of our physical lives, judging by the previous paragraphs) depend on the quality and strength of our social networks and what runs through the veins of that network. In his words, "We form social networks because the benefits of a connected life outweigh the costs. If I were always violent toward you ... or made you sad ... you would cut the ties to me and the network would disintegrate. So the spread of good and valuable things is required to sustain and nourish social networks. Similarly, social networks are required for the spread of good and valuable things like love, and kindness, and happiness, and altruism, and ideas. ...I think social networks are fundamentally related to goodness, and what I think the world needs now is more connections."[63]

INFORMATION, AWARENESS, AND HEALING

In addition to contemplating the value of mutual guarantee, thus increasing its "popularity," we need to contemplate ways of inculcating it through action. One such possibility is to bring as many experts, such as Christakis, Fowler, and others, under an umbrella organization that will make these ideas available through the education system, the media, and via popular entertainment.

The manner in which these ideas will be expressed should be left to the professionals in each field, just as musicians and filmmakers express their ideas today. Every person consumes different kinds of media, entertainment, and information. People already know what they like to watch and read, and where they like to go. Some people like to watch TV at home, some in the gym, and some in the bar. Some don't like TV at all, but consume their information and entertainment through the internet. All of that may remain the same, but what does need to *gradually* change is the kind of content these outlets present.

Currently, they present a wealth of information, most of which we are not even aware that we are consuming. We simply enjoy reading or watching it without thinking too much about it. Within the media, however, are people such as advertisers who skillfully implant their ideas in our minds—such as that one company is better than another, or that without the newest gadget in the market our lives will not be worth calling a "life." While these ideas are false, they sink into our minds and trouble our thoughts until we ease our minds by buying the advertised item.

Now, consider what would happen t if our minds were implanted with the idea that we are all interconnected, and that hurting others is just like hurting yourself. What would it be like if the world followed the motto— "If you're not good, you're no good"?

But not only the media needs to change. If schools taught "Connectivity Classes," if you could major in "practical interconnectedness" at university, or coach "prosocial networking" to individuals and company staffs, a whole new social atmosphere, a new buzz of connectedness would emerge. Within a few months, people would come to feel that there was a genuine alternative to self-centeredness—one that offered greater value for a lower cost.

Everything would change. Instead of ordering others around, idea sharing would be the way to connect with co-workers and peers at school. Personal tests at schools and universities would become obsolete because a person's skill would not depend on the extent to which one could memorize answers. Instead, one's value would be a reflection of the extent to which one was *connected*, on the level to which one has developed channels of information. In such a state, a personal test would be irrelevant; a group assignment would be a far more appropriate means of evaluation.

In addition to the changes at work or school, our social lives will be transformed. When connectedness is key to one's success and happiness, what one cultivates is one's connections. Connections are made not only at work, but to a great extent during our "off duty" hours. As a result, attending outings, socializing, playing, and deliberating would become far more popular because they would not have a mere recreational value, but would be regarded as a contribution to one's *entire* life.

At work, too, the atmosphere would be far more sociable, as socializing would be a tool for personal and professional advancement. Moreover, an appreciation of our interdependence and the importance of positive social connections would diminish the frequency of unfair or unjust behavior at work. As Christakis mentioned in his above-mentioned lecture, "If I were always violent toward you ... or made you sad ... you would cut the ties to me and the network would disintegrate." This would be counterproductive to one's personal and professional advancement.

The fundamental concept is simple: We are all interconnected, hence interdependent. Therefore, we must solve our problems in the spirit of mutual guarantee, where all are guarantors of each other's well-being.

If, for instance, a company decided it needed to improve its business performance and make it suitable for the globalized world, the company would ask a mutual guarantee coach to train staff (employers and employees alike) to work and think "as a company" in an interconnected world. The results would be improved interpersonal connections, a better flow of information throughout the company, a greater degree of trust at all levels, and a more thorough examination of each stage in the design and production of products, thus yielding better products and enhancing customer relations.

EMPLOYMENT AND TRAINING

"Science may never come up with a better office communication system than the coffee break."

Attributed to Earl Wilson

The need to cultivate new connections in the human society will help us cope even with the rising problem of global unemployment. The heads of the Organization for Economic Co-operation and Development (OECD) and the International Labor Organization (ILO) recently stated that "The overall number of unemployed is still at 200 million worldwide, close to the peak recorded at the depth of the Great Recession."[64] Even in the G20 countries, the warning continued, "The analysis ... expresses concern that employment may ... grow ... until the end of 2012, resulting in a 40 million job shortfall in G20 countries next year [2012] and a much larger shortfall by 2015."

According to the *Huffington Post*, "Spain's unemployment rate rose sharply to a new Eurozone high of 21.3 percent in the first quarter of the year [2011], with a record 4.9 million people out of work,"[65] and the

U.S. Bureau of Labor Statistics reported that the current unemployment rate in the U.S. is 8.6, with 13.3 million people out of work.[66]

However, most alarming and most socially volatile is the unemployment rate of youths in the Eurozone, particularly in Spain and Greece, but also in the United States. A December 22, 2011 news item by Felix Salmon for Reuters reports, "Spain and Greece have almost unthinkably high youth unemployment approaching 50%, but also that Ireland … has seen its youth unemployment rate go through the roof since the crisis, from below 10% to over 30%."[67]

Regarding the U.S., the story continues, "The thing to note here is not just the absolute level—youth unemployment is now 18.1%, and for blacks it's 31%—but also the sharp rise [from just over 10 in 2007 to just over 18 in 2010]."

Without explicitly saying it, the report offers a grim comparison whose meaning is crystal clear: "The U.S. is in exactly the same ballpark as the levels we saw in the Middle East which caused the Arab Spring. We're lower than Egypt and Tunisia, but we're higher than Morocco and Syria."

Young, educated people feel that they spent their best years and the best of their resources (or their parents' resources) to become qualified for a world that no longer exists. That assessment is not just a gut feeling. In his book, *The Brave New World of Work*, Professor Ulrich Beck, one of Europe's leading sociologists, explains that "The work society is coming to an end as more and more people are ousted by smart technologies. To our counterparts at the end of the 21st century, today's struggles over jobs will seem like a fight over deckchairs on the Titanic. The 'job for life' has disappeared ... and all paid work is subject to the threat of replacement."[68]

Whether we want it or not, the crisis will lead to a reduction of redundant industries and to the recognition that most of the world's population is simply not needed in the job market. Yet, if people are not working now and will not work in the future, what should they do? How will they live? And if they are provided for by the government or some other agency, wouldn't being idle all day destroy them mentally and emotionally? This could be an explosive situation for any society, a constant cause of unrest, disorder, and crime.

The solution to human idleness will be to send people back to school. However, this will not be high school all over again, nor college, nor even adult education of any kind we know. It will be a "Globalization School for Citizens of the Interconnected World." Studies at that school will not cost money. On the contrary, the school will grant its participants scholarships, just as university students receive grants and scholarships. The state will finance the grants with the money it will save as it cuts the civil service work force, since unemployment benefits cost the state less than keeping people employed in hidden unemployment.

Also, the growing awareness of our interconnectedness will create an atmosphere in which it will be easier for the "haves" to share some of what they have with the "have-nots." Some adjustment in taxation is also likely, even if it's simply in the form of collecting real taxes, rather than the rich evading them through sophisticated accounting. Again, all these changes must happen *willingly*, once a large majority in society recognizes our interconnectedness and interdependence and *wishes* to live accordingly.

Sharing does not have to come in the form of money: it may well present itself in the forms of offering inexpensive houses for rent, narrowing profit margins on staple products to help the less affluent, and numerous other means by which one can show one's support of society.

The reason why the payment for participation in the Globalization School will be considered a grant and not unemployment benefits is that unemployment benefits can carry a negative social tag, while grants do not. It is very important that students at the new school feel confident and even proud of being there. This will make them much more receptive to the material being taught.

At the Globalization School, people will learn how to handle themselves in a world that has become interconnected, where they are dependent on others for their sustenance. They will learn about the course of evolution as discussed earlier in this book, the necessity to adjust human society to that course, the benefits from adjusting, and the harms from delaying the adjustment. People will learn the value of communication, new ways to communicate, and will acquire down-to-earth skills such as home economics and interpersonal communication, and other necessary knowledge for times of rapid change.

Because people will have much more leisure time, they will be able to use it to learn new skills. These skills will be taught at the school but will also be useful outside of it, giving people more options when searching for a job—as opportunities to socialize with new people, or by opening new avenues to contribute to society. Any skill with real merit, be it farming or computer programming, will be useful in the future as it is today. Because people's livelihood will not depend on their ability to sell their products, they will focus on developing only what is really needed and helpful. They will manufacture products that are built to last, rather than products with planned obsolescence, intended to force people to spend more than they should or would like.

People will now have time for socializing. They will still attend school or work, but there will be a lot more free time than there is today, and people will use it to socialize, as we discussed earlier in this chapter. Socializing will not be a goal in and of itself, but a means for enrichment, a learning aid, a chance to gain insights into new realms of knowledge, new depths of thought, or simply to enhance personal confidence by having more friends (real friends, not Facebook friends).

Looking ahead, a few years from now life will be very different. Today people are so stressed they hardly have time to breathe. We are living in a constant rat race on an ever-spinning, ever accelerating wheel. But when the industry contracts and we do not need to work as many hours, we will have more time to cultivate our interests and our social ties. It is then that we will experience real growth and the growth of happiness.

In his *The New York Times* column, "The Earth is Full,"[69] Thomas Friedman, author of *The World is Flat: A brief history of the twenty-first century*, discusses Paul Gilding's book, *The Great Disruption: Why the Climate Crisis Will Bring On the End of Shopping and the Birth of a New World*. Friedman quotes Gilding as saying, "If you cut down more trees than you grow, you run out of trees." As the impact of the imminent Great Disruption hits us, Gilding writes, "Our response will be proportionally dramatic, mobilizing as we do in war. We will change at a scale and speed we can barely imagine today, completely transforming our economy, including our energy and transportation industries, in just a few short decades."

Friedman explains that according to Gilding, we will realize that the consumer-driven growth model is broken and we must move to a more happiness-driven growth model, based on people working less and owning less. "How many people," Gilding asks, "lie on their death bed and say, 'I wish I had worked harder or built more shareholder value,' and how many say, 'I wish I had gone to more ballgames, read more books to my kids, taken more walks?' To do that, you need a growth model based on giving people more time to enjoy life, but with less stuff."

THE PRINCIPLES OF EDUCATION

"To repair the world means to repair education."[70]
Janusz Korczak, an educator

So far, we've talked about the adult society in general and adult education in particular. However, in the long run, our future depends on how we educate our children, not ourselves. For this reason, it seems appropriate to introduce some of the fundamentals of children's education in the new world.

First and foremost is the school. The purpose of the school in the new world is not merely to inculcate knowledge just so a child will pass a test. Rather, the school should rear children into being human, or better yet, *humane*. Children should be educated about the kind of world in which they will be living when they become adults. They should be given the tools to be the connected and communicative persons we aspire to teach adults to be, able to construct genuine and lasting relations of mutual guarantee.

This will be accomplished by setting up a prosocial environment at school, and—very important—a pro-school environment at home. Instead of being taught how to be the best in their class, children need to be taught how to build a society where all children are connected to one another, where the atmosphere is one of friendship and equality. They can begin, for example, by sitting in circles instead of in rows next to separate desks. They can be taught through games that reveal how much power and sense of belonging this form of study offers.

The concept of social learning, rather than individual learning, is not a theoretical notion. It has been tried numerous times with repeated success, to the point that one must wonder how we could have been oblivious to its obvious advantages for so long.

In an essay called, "An Educational Psychology Success Story: Social Interdependence Theory and Cooperative Learning," University of Minnesota professors, David W. Johnson and Roger T. Johnson present a compelling case for the "social interdependence" theory. In their words, "More than 1,200 research studies have been conducted in the past 11 decades on cooperative, competitive, and individualistic efforts."[71]

Johnson and Johnson compared the effectiveness of cooperative learning to the commonly used individual, competitive learning. The results were unequivocal. In terms of individual accountability and personal responsibility, they concluded, "The positive interdependence that binds group members together is posited to result in feelings of responsibility for (a) completing one's share of the work and (b) facilitating the work of other group members. Furthermore, when a person's performance affects the outcomes of collaborators, the person feels responsible for the collaborators' welfare as well as for his or her own. Failing oneself is bad, but failing others as well as oneself is worse."[72]

In other words, positive interdependence turns individualists into caring and collaborative people, the complete opposite of the current trend where excessive individualism reaches the level of narcissism.

To demonstrate the benefits of collaboration, the researchers measured the achievements of students who collaborated compared to those who competed. "The average person cooperating was found to achieve at about two thirds of a standard deviation above the average person performing within a competitive or individualistic situation."[73]

To understand the meaning of such a deviation above the average, consider that if a child is a D-average student, by cooperating, his or her grades will leap to an astonishing A+ average. Also, they wrote, "Cooperation, when compared with competitive and individualistic efforts, tends to promote greater long-term retention, higher intrinsic motivation and expectations for success, more creative thinking ... and more positive attitudes toward the task and school."[74]

In collaborative learning, the teacher's role is not to dictate the material, but above all, to guide the children. They should perceive their teacher as a grownup friend, as well as a knowledgeable person. Teachers and students should sit together in a circle, at equal heights, and discuss as equals. Here, superiority and control are replaced with subtle guidance to help children discover things for themselves, through deliberation or through their group efforts.

Children learn to deliberate, to share views and to argue, while still respecting one another for their personal merits and uniqueness. This allows each of them to express his or her thoughts freely and reveal each student's special qualities. In this way, children will expand their worldview and absorb new ideas and perspectives.

By repeating this mode of learning, children learn to appreciate the connection between them as their most important asset, as this is what grants them all the knowledge and power they possess. They begin to enjoy succeeding only together with others, and each person's worth is measured not by individual excellence, but by the contribution of one's excellence to the group's success.

The study groups will be relatively small, and each group will be joined by one or two children who are two to three years older than them. These older children will serve as instructors. Because of a child's natural inclination to copy older children, these child-instructors will actually be the best teachers, as students will naturally try to imitate them. The older children who teach also have much to gain—a deeper understanding of the material, a deeper understanding of themselves, and an opportunity to contribute to society and win its approbation.

Disciplining children will be treated very differently than in today's schools. When there is a case of misconduct, the children themselves, together with the adults and professionals, will decide how to handle the situation. Children must be taught constructive critical thinking, and analyzing moments of small crises are great opportunities for teaching such thinking. If one child misbehaves, the class will congregate and discuss what should be done about it, and how to prevent it from recurring.

The discussion would not be a theoretical process. Rather, children (not the ones being discussed) will simulate the situation and report to the class how they felt, what drove them to behave as they did, and so on. They will then conduct a group discussion where all the children take part, so that once a decision has been reached, all the children will actually have "experienced" being all parties in the incident. They can thus make a decision in a much more just, yet compassionate and understanding manner.

Such discussions teach children to consider issues from different angles, and to know that it's okay and even natural to have many views on the same issue. Moreover, through repeated simulation and examination of ideas from different viewpoints, children will learn to expect to change their minds, have regrets, admit mistakes, and justify their friends' views rather than their own.

At least once a week, children will go on outings and tours to help them know the world they live in from "up close." Recommended outings would include places they would usually not get to see and learn about, such as banks, police headquarters, museums of all kinds, factories, and courts.

Each such outing will be preceded by explanations about the place they are going to visit, what they expect to find, what they already know about that place, its role in their lives and how well it performs its role, how it benefits society, what kind of people work there, and what kind of training and schooling one needs in order to work there. After the tour the children will discuss and share their experiences and lessons from the outing, thus enriching one another with their insights.

Through these tours and outings children will come to know the world in a much more personal manner than just by seeing it on TV, where they would be influenced by the perspective that the director wishes to show. Sometimes, as with museums, children will not know at all about these places were it not for the school. Beyond learning about the place that they visit, by knowing the elements that affect their lives they will come to feel firsthand the mesh that connects human society.

They will learn that the world is integrated and connected through "hands on" experiences, by simply showing different places, their functions in our lives, and their connections to other places that affect their lives. This information is vital to a child's confidence and preparation for life beyond school.

Another important learning aid is the video camera. It is recommended that all lessons—which are not "lessons" but are discussions and group work—be documented on video. Children quickly become used to the presence of the camera and will behave naturally. This allows them to see themselves from the side by replaying events that require special attention. Looking at a video of a situation, they can analyze more clearly how they worked as a group, how they dealt with interferences, and how they related to one another. Accordingly, they can judge themselves and their relations with others and see where they are successful and where they need to improve.[75]

PUSHING FOR THE CHANGE TOGETHER

> "We are by no means strangers, and we are linked by a common destiny. And these turbulent times must bind us ever closer together."
> Christine Lagarde, Managing Director, International Monetary Fund[76]

All the changes we have described so far in both the adult and the children's societies will create a new atmosphere in our surroundings. As we could see, these changes will affect every part of our lives—work, family, friends, school, the judicial system, the media, interpersonal relations, international relations, trade relations, and so forth.

Interestingly, we do not need all of society to set this transformation in motion, but a relatively small number of people. Scientists at the prestigious Rensselaer Polytechnic Institute (RPI) discovered that even when only 10 percent of the population shares a conviction or belief, the rest of society adopts it. The mathematical models show that there is a sudden leap in acceptance: below 10 percent, the effect is barely discernible, but once the 10 percent mark is reached, the view spreads like a wildfire.[77]

Considering that the internet in general, and social networks in particular, enable the rapid spread of ideas, it is enough that we begin to talk about the need to connect above all differences for the future of all of us, and invoke as many people as possible into that notion. The scientists at RPI gave Tunisia and Egypt as examples for such a process, saying, "In those countries, dictators who were in power for decades were suddenly overthrown in just a few weeks."

When you think about it, there are likely far more than 10 percent who want to have a safer, friendlier world than the one we have now, so the chances of making 10 percent of the population adamant about it, thus instigating the shift, are far higher than may appear at first glance.

CAMPAIGNING FOR OUR LIVES

Mutual guarantee is like a sphere that grows by connecting opposites. True, we are different in every way—in our thoughts, our habits, our characters, and in our bodies. But at the same time, we understand that reality dictates that we unite and work together. A society that projects the message that mutual guarantee is the fundamental law of life will make us not only understand this concept intellectually, but will strive to implement it in our daily lives. Just as good advertising creates such a buzz around a new product or service that we feel compelled to buy it, creating a buzz around the concept of mutual guarantee will make us feel that we just have to have it, have to feel what it's like to live that way.

A systematic and consistent building of a society with global thinking will make each of us develop an inclusive perception of the world. Instead of "me" and "them," we will begin to see reality as "we" or "all of us." We will shift from wanting personal gratification to wanting gratification for the general populace. Our viewpoint will expand from personal to collective, and new insights will evoke within us.

> "Multiplicity is only apparent. In truth, there is only one mind."
>
> Erwin Schrödinger, physicist, one of the founders of quantum mechanics[78]

SOCIAL JUSTICE

"The West is being challenged to deliver not
just growth, but inclusive growth, which, most
critically, involves greater social justice."

Mohamed A. El-Erian, CEO of PIMCO,
and author of *When Markets Collide*[79]

The global social unrest of 2011 presented a serious
challenge. On the one hand, the demand to have
a decent living standard for all is understandable.
On the other hand, governments cannot break their
budgets if they are to maintain functional economies.
In days when virtually the entire world is in a deep
economic crisis whose end is nowhere in sight, when
many countries are in danger of imminent insolvency,
it is irresponsible to increase budgets, which are already
in deep deficit. Yet, people are demanding social justice,
and rightly so. So what should governments do?

First, it is important to keep in mind that, as Einstein said, "The significant problems we face cannot be solved at the same level of thinking that was used when we created them."[80]

Boaz Schwartz, CEO of the Deutsche Bank delegation in Israel, said in a special panel summoned by the Israeli financial newspaper, *Globes*, "We mustn't underestimate the intense social emotions we are seeing. These emotions will have vast repercussions in the coming years. We must prepare for a world of social concepts, of equal sharing of revenue, and different pricing... Countries that will fail to adjust themselves accordingly will find themselves in a tough spot; their economies will suffer."[81]

We should also keep in mind that the economy reflects the nature of our relations with each other, which is then "translated" into monetary relations. The division of resources in society and the socioeconomic ideology at its foundation derive from the values of society and from the relations among its members. This is why economy is not a law of Nature or a hard science such as physics or chemistry.

This is why Joseph Stiglitz, winner of the Nobel Prize in economy, said at the beginning of his lecture at the 2011 Lindau Nobel Laureate Meeting in Economic Sciences: "The test of any science is prediction. And if you can't predict something as important as a global financial crisis or the magnitude of the one that we are going through, obviously something's wrong with your model."[82]

Likewise, the governor of the Bank of Israel and former first deputy director of the International Monetary Fund (IMF), Stanley Fischer, said in a video interview with CNBC's Senior Economics Reporter, Steve Liesman, "We're in very difficult territory. This is not where the textbooks five years ago would have expected us to be. ...You're operating under extreme conditions and the textbooks aren't quite sure what to do in those cases."[83]

When we move toward the social, communicational, and educational changes described in the previous chapter, we will be able to construct a new, inclusive concept of economics, one that is founded on social concern and is in sync with the laws of the new world. The decision-making processes and their execution, the structure of the socioeconomic system, the links between decision-makers and those who carry out those decisions will be done with a sense of mutual guarantee.

In other words, the right order of operations to guarantee our sustainable well-being begins with an explanation of the need for mutual guarantee, for education for living in the new world. The social and economic systems will be redefined and reconstructed based on that need. In the meantime, until those definitions are provided and the reconstruction executed, we should conduct round-table type discussions, where all participants are of equal status, and together agree on the type of assistance those who are less affluent require for basic sustenance.

We will elaborate on how to achieve that agreement through round-table discussions in a moment, but first it is important to note that such a division of funds will not be sufficient in and of itself for securing our well-being. The concern for others' well-being dictates that we endow all people with a minimal ability to conduct respectable living. These funds, along with training in personal finance (home economics), will enable us to proceed with society's healing process.

ACHIEVING AGREEMENT

Representatives from all factions of society should assemble in round-table discussions. They will have a heavy burden of responsibility—operating as "heads" of the human family. Without the sense that all of humanity is a single family, the representatives at the table will not succeed in arriving at just decisions.

Another necessary condition for the success of the discussions will be transparency. All deliberations must be broadcast live, including the quarrels, disputes, and the hard decision-making processes. Everything should unfold right before the eyes of the entire world. In a sense, it will be a new kind of reality show, but one whose consequences will affect each and every one of us, all the members of the human family. And just like a reality show, the viewers will have a say in the final decisions.

In our actual reality, the viewers, all of us, will also be seated at the table. People will have to decide on priorities. This will be a prolonged process that will require everyone's participation and involvement. Clearly, it will not be a simple exercise, but because we are rebuilding our society from scratch, there will be no other way. Only when we include the entire human family in the decisions will we be able to consider ourselves a true family.

Studies indicate that when one is involved in the decision-making process, his or her involvement invokes a positive, caring attitude toward that process, whatever decision is reached. In other words, even when the final decision benefits other sectors of society before one's own, people who were involved in making that decision are likely to support it, even if they did not initially approve of it.[84] Thus, the sense that citizens are being ignored by decision-makers, who are subject to the pressure of lobbyists, will be replaced with a feeling of social solidarity and trust.

In fact, the round-table *modus operandi* should be our mode of action in all our decisions. It should become part of the management paradigm of society and state. In the course of our lives, we will often have frequent discussions regarding our problems, weighing them, grading them, prioritizing them, and together deciding on how to solve them. The round table is a perfect means to teach us how to truly become a single family.

However, and this is important, seeing everyone—on the levels of city, state, or world—as a single family does not mean we should give up our views. On the contrary, all views and approaches have merit. The recognition that we are all a family dictates that we understand that others with different views also have a place in the family. But even more than that, we should regard differing views as a constant source of enrichment. They provide new perspectives, new approaches to solving problems, and new information that we could not have come to know were it not for views that are different from ours.

Raising the value of public benefit will help each of us relinquish our own views when necessary. Once we present our views, and then recognize that another's view better serves the public interest, we will accept that other view. Just as in a family, the collective interest overrides all else.

Indeed, why can't the world be like a family? Is this not the real meaning of social justice? Is there any other way to achieve and sustain it?

The beginning of this new worldview will likely not be a smooth ride. Differences and hurdles are to be expected. Nevertheless, as we see that process through to achieve genuine consensus, we will learn that an open discussion enables us to work out our differences and achieve broad agreement. Indeed, the round table is not merely a notion of open discussion among equal peers. It is also an educational process on national and international levels of unprecedented scope.

THE BENEFITS OF MUTUAL GUARANTEE

As explained above, the new world dictates that we adopt the approach of mutual guarantee. At first glance, mutual guarantee may seem like a naïve notion, impractical in real life. However, implementing the mutual guarantee approach has very real implications in society and in the economy. Below, we will note three of the most obvious implications: a positive social climate, increased surpluses, and diminished costs of living. You will find a detailed explanation of the favorable implications of the mutual guarantee economy in the Appendix, "Benefits of the New Economy."

1. **A positive social climate:** One's very engagement in positive social values will create a positive atmosphere, which is mandatory for any growth. A new spirit will fill the air, and the heart will be filled with hope for a brighter, better future. In a society that encourages such values as solidarity and mutual consideration, a sense of genuine trust among us will gradually form. That sensation does not depend on personal wealth, but rather on knowing that others care about us. Only in such a supportive environment will we be able to stop fearing that we are being used, or that others are "out to get us." With fear and anxiety for our future and that of our children all but gone, we will be able to truly grow and prosper.

2. **Increasing surpluses:** The mutual guarantee will increase surpluses. Consider how much "stuff" we have at home that we do not need.

When every person, business, city council, and government feels like part of a collective "family," huge surpluses will surface in food, goods, and services. These can be transferred for others to use, and monetary surpluses will be used to cover some of the current demands. This will significantly alleviate the need to increase budgets or taxes.

Another point is that municipalities will not struggle for public funds because the mindset of "I have to take care of my interests because no one else will" will be obsolete, as everyone will feel responsible for everyone else's well-being. Therefore, municipalities will not ask for more than they need and will not keep reserves in "hidden corners" of the budget through accounting wizardry. Instead, they will contemplate how to help one another, thus making vast resources immediately available.

3. **Lowering costs of living:** Today, the price of goods and services is determined by businesses that aspire to maximize their own profits. Elevating the importance of mutual guarantee in public discourse will impel these businesses to be more considerate of the public interest, and this will lead to lower prices for all.

    If public appreciation is withheld from those who made the most money and is refocused on those who contributed the most to society, the natural drive for approbation will direct businesses toward more prosocial behaviors.

In his story, "Why Doing Good Is Good for Business,"[85] Richard McGill Murphy, contributor to *CNN Money*, mentioned the case of the drug giant Pfizer giving away drugs. This story demonstrates the positive effect that public approbation or admonition can have on a business. According to McGill Murphy, "As unemployment crept toward 10% last year [2009], the drug giant Pfizer decided to do a good deed. For customers who had lost their jobs during 2009 and lacked prescription coverage, Pfizer would supply 70 of its name-brand drugs ... free of charge for up to a year. For a company whose reputation has suffered some blemishes, including $2.3 billion in fines last year for improperly marketing drugs to doctors, the free-prescription program was well worth the cost. 'We did it because we thought it was the right thing to do,' says Pfizer CEO Jeffrey Kindler. 'But it was motivational for our employees and got a great response from customers. In the long run it will help our business.'"

All that has been said above shows that mutual guarantee is not an abstract notion, but a very practical concept that produces substantial income for all. Mutual guarantee creates social and economic value, and holds the key to our problems on the social, economic, and political levels.

When there is evidence of inequality, there arises the demand for social justice. Our egos will never allow us feel inferior to others, disrespected, degraded, or worthless. Such distress cannot be resolved by money alone; it requires a more inclusive, humane approach. If we can not build a society where all are equally important, where all genuinely listen to one another and care for one another, where everyone truly has an equal opportunity for dignified living, the bitterness within will explode, as the bloody examples of the "Arab Spring" have demonstrated.

Our future is at stake, and the solution lies in changing our social values and healing our relationships with each other, whether on a personal level or between citizens and state. The mutual guarantee approach will lead us to true social justice, and therefore holds the key to our sustainability and prosperity. Mutual guarantee will not only bring us economic and financial security, it will restore our confidence in life and the peace of mind and happiness that have been absent in our world for so many decades.

Part Two

Building a New Society – Points to Consider

A recap and new perspectives on the principles presented in Part One

CRISIS AND OPPORTUNITY

NEW LAWS

Imagine yourself driving your car when it suddenly begins to choke and shudder. At first, it's only one system that breaks down, but then another and another follow. It's not that the car has completely shut down. The main systems, like the engine and the gear, are still running. But the lights go on and off intermittently, and every so often the car jerks to a halt. Then, miraculously, the failing engine restarts.

Yes, you're still moving but the odds are not good that you'll continue moving much longer. If this happened to you, what would you do?

In much the same way, our entire world is gradually becoming dysfunctional. There are breakdowns everywhere, but we are still gamely pulling forward, despite the warnings of experts. They tell us that, in the current state of affairs, we must do an overhaul or the whole machine of humanity will come to a complete standstill, at an enormous cost. If the economy continues to deteriorate, the nearly 50 million Americans living on food stamps will multiply many times over, and many others will suffer real hunger all over the world, not just in the poorest countries, as today.

The crisis that's jolting the world is reality's way of informing us that we aren't running it properly. We have built a system of banks, industry, and international relations that have gone out of our control. We are learning that the Keynesian principles of embedded self-interest and invisible hand no longer keep our selfishness in check. Like a spreading cancer, we are destroying our planet, as well as our society.

NOWHERE TO RUN

In a global economic crisis, each country tends to think, "How good would it be if we could separate ourselves from the rest of the world, have all our needs for the sustenance of our citizens provided by ourselves, and be completely self-sufficient just as we were a hundred years ago or so? Why don't we turn back the wheel, set up high tariffs to impede import, trade with other countries only where we are totally incapable of providing for ourselves, and freeze all business partnerships with overseas companies? Yes, the standard of living may drop, but we would be less dependent on others."

We don't understand that there is no way back from globalization. We can no longer separate ourselves from the rest of the world. Globalization and interdependence are here to stay. Cutting ourselves off would be like cutting an organ from a living organism in order to be saved from an illness that has afflicted the rest of the organism. If you cut off a finger, would it survive without the body from which it came?

A BOOMERANG

At first glance, mutual guarantee may seem utopian, too naïve a concept to work in our self-centered world. But in fact, life is now compelling us to adopt it!

Throughout history we have progressed by acting on the drives that arose within us. We constantly felt a need to do something, to change the status quo. We waged wars, fought in revolutions, and rebelled. We have advanced and grown through conflicts and struggles, but the price we paid was destruction.

Today, when we are interdependent, wars and struggles will not solve our problems. Brute force cannot mend the world. A connected world cannot be run with an egoistic mindset propagated by oppression and forced governance. The rule is simple: If we are interdependent, then whatever one person does to others returns like a boomerang, and just as sharply and powerfully. If we understand that all connected systems operate this way, we will succeed.

ACCELERATING EXPONENTIALLY

Time seems to be compressing. In the 20th century, humanity experienced more than it had in all of human history preceding it. The 21st century began only recently, and already much has happened.

We are living in exponential times, and the pace of life is accelerating accordingly. While there will be more hectic times and less hectic times, the trend is unmistakable. The pace of change is evident everywhere— we change our jobs more frequently (assuming we have one), we change our spouses more frequently (assuming we have one), and we change our houses more frequently (again, assuming we have one).

But where the pace of change is most clearly evident is technology. Look at your cell phone and compare it to the phones we were using only 40 years ago. If you consider that today's average cell phone is thousands of times more powerful than the Apollo 11 computer— which landed the spaceship on the moon—it is easy to see just how quickly and radically we are changing.

A COMMON SOLUTION

The multiple crises facing humanity indicate that we need to take an inclusive approach to solving them. In an interconnected world, there is no such thing as a local problem. The need for solutions that favor all of humanity will call for consistent deliberation among representatives of all countries as equals. Each side would present the problems it considers urgent, and then every problem would be weighed to see in which order it should be addressed. Only by deliberating in the spirit of our connection in a global web will we find the right way to solve these problems.

The alternative to deliberation is far less appealing—war.

WHY BOND?

Many experts already understand that it is impossible for any country to overcome the global crisis on its own. However, Nature's course of evolution, as explained in Chapter 2, raises another point: cooperation and collaboration must be undertaken not only because no country can solve the crisis alone, but because this is the course of the whole of evolution. This global crisis is an opportunity for us to discover it and unite into a single organism, just as the whole of Nature does naturally.

NATURAL DEVELOPMENT

NATURE DOESN'T TOLERATE IMBALANCE

Nature doesn't tolerate imbalance. Heat moves from hotter to colder to even out the temperature; air pressure is balanced by wind; water flows to lower ground until it evens out the higher level from which it flowed. In every place, in every phenomenon, Nature strives for balance.

Another example is our body-temperature control mechanism: Temperature receptors are dispersed throughout the human body and update the information-processing center in the brain (hypothalamus) on any change in the surrounding atmosphere. The brain then sends orders to effectors such as sweat glands and muscles, which secrete sweat, contract, or shiver, thus maintaining the body temperature. In this way, the body balances the heat that it generates with the heat that it loses, maintaining body temperature at a constant 37°C (98.6°F).

Nature's imperative to bring everything into balance is beginning to affect humanity. The unrest and protests that we see throughout the world are expressions of our need for balance on the human level. While we are all different as individuals, the criterion for balance is the same for us all: we must support one another; there is no other way. Whether we want to or not, Nature's way will win and we will have to comply. The only question is at what cost.

THE BENEFITS OF UNITY

Today, everything we do requires energy and effort on our part. If we are in balance, we need hardly make any effort to obtain anything. Instead, we are in a state of ease, where anyplace we go, everyone is ready to help us with whatever we need. In turn, we are ready to reciprocate. Everything flows easily, we waste much less energy, and encounter far fewer obstacles.

In every realm of life, being in balance clears resistance. This applies to interpersonal relations, as well as anything we produce from Nature. Through unity among us, we will bring the whole of Nature to inclusive balance and will lack nothing. There will be abundance everywhere.

GLOBAL HUNGER IS NOT A MUST

Our planet can feed far more people than Earth's current population, provided we do not interfere with Nature, and provided we unite like organs in a single organism.

GREATER THAN TOYS

The next step in evolution is not a new species (although that, too, may happen). The significant new stage of evolution is actually a shift in human consciousness. In this process we must gradually develop our awareness and understanding; we must build the analysis-synthesis mechanism of reality. We must figure out how our planet operates, who we are, and what our approach to life should be. We are living in special times. If we succeed in opening our eyes, softening our hearts, and expanding our awareness, we will be able to move through this stage quickly, successfully, and easily.

SOCIAL SOLIDARITY

WHY THEM INSTEAD OF ME?

Besides the demand for a more even division of wealth, people feel bitter about any inequalities, including the lack of equal opportunities. However, the truth is that no just division will help until we develop a social awareness that supports mutual guarantee. Favoring one sector of the population over another will only trigger anger and bitterness among other sectors. Without the mindset of mutual guarantee, people who will not be on the receiving end will always feel resentment and will ask themselves, "Why them and not me?"

WHAT IS MUTUAL GUARANTEE?

Mutual guarantee is a reciprocal connection requiring that we consider everyone as if they were our closest kin.

We may find it hard to believe that this is possible, but the evolution of human society will lead us to a state where we will feel the whole world within us, similar to the way we feel our kin. We will feel who among our kin needs help and what kind of help they need—whether the need concerns aged parents, small children, unexpected expenses and payments, ill health, etc.. Naturally, we prioritize our family's needs according to urgency. Would we neglect an ailing grandfather? Not if we are a normal family. The sense of commitment, of mutual guarantee, compels us to be that way. This is how we must approach our relationships with the rest of humanity.

WHAT IS EQUALITY?

Equality is a state in which each of us possesses equal opportunities and personal possibilities for constructive self expression in the collective system—to give and to receive, to be balanced with the rest of humanity.

For example, the heart is equal to the lungs; the lungs are equal to the liver; the liver is equal to the kidneys, which are equal to the legs, which are equal to the hands...

In what are they equal? They all operate in reciprocity for the body's benefit. However, each part of the body focuses on different functions required for the well-being of the entire body. This is what keeps us (the organism) alive and healthy.

Similarly, if one person belongs to one part of humanity, it doesn't make him or her any less worthy than another person from another part. To paraphrase, I may belong to the "heart" of humanity and someone else may belong to the "brain" of humanity, or to humanity's "liver." These are conditions into which we were born and which were predetermined for us. But to sustain the health and well-being of humanity, we must work together as equals *where we were positioned*, and not regard ourselves as superior or inferior because we were positioned in one place and not in another.

We are all born to different families, with different genes, and different upbringing. Our worldviews may be very different and we may also feel different from each other. But if each of us feels in harmony with others, we will achieve equality.

THE MOVER, THE GEEK, AND EQUALITY

Let's assume that we have two people: one is a 6'5" hulking mover working 12 hours a day, and the other is a 5'1" weedy computer geek. The mover makes $15 an hour plus tips, and the geek, whose furniture he is moving today, makes $150 an hour, plus bonuses and options. Is this fair?

One was given strength, another was given brains. They both use what they were given by Nature with equal diligence, so why should one make more than the other? They both contribute what they can and what they do best to society, so in their contribution, they are equal. Why doesn't this apply to their salaries?

Let's change the description a little. What if the mover and the geek were brothers? Would the geek still be oblivious to his brother's financial hardship? Even better, what if the geek were the mover's father? Would he let his son go hungry or broke just because he didn't get his father's brains but a bulky physique instead?

Today, the mindset that we are all equal when we expend equal efforts is the only one that can keep our society intact. The way toward that mindset is by consistently reeducating ourselves until we have absorbed the reality that we are all actually kin. Once we place mutual guarantee at the top of our priority list, we will discover that the world has suddenly become a place where life can truly be easy and joyful.

A NEW SOCIAL LADDER

What can make us naturally self-centered humans put the public's benefit above our own? Only the influence of the environment! Therefore, we must change our social values so that people are appreciated for their contribution to society, not according to the size of their bank accounts. When will life be good on this planet? It will happen when we all think not of ourselves first, but after everyone else.

Appendices

Previous Publications by the ARI Institute

WE, WE, WE

That we are in the midst of a "global crisis" is no longer in question. Since there is also ample evidence that the term "globalization" covers far more than the correlation between global financial markets, a more accurate meaning of the term should address the interconnected nature of society as a whole. We are "global" not just in the financial sense, but also, if not primarily, in the social, if not emotional sense. Our emotions affect those of other people so intensely that they can start social blazes in country after country, passing from one hot spot to the next via the wires that connect the World Wide Web.

The "Arab Spring" has expanded far beyond the Arab world. In each country, the causes and the manifestations of the protests wear a different "attire." In Egypt, mass demonstrations overthrew the government. In Syria, the people's heroic resistance in the face of carnage is a testimony to the profound spiritual change that has arisen. Citizens simply cannot tolerate tyranny any longer.

In Israel, demonstrations are peaceful but of an unprecedented magnitude. In the demonstration that took place on Saturday, August 6, 2011, 300,000 people participated, roughly one out of every 22 Israelis. If one out of 22 Americans were to participate in a demonstration, it would require space for roughly 14 million people.

In Spain, the tent camps of protestors have been standing for months, with neither a solution nor dispersion of the camp dwellers in sight. In the U.K., violent riots have erupted that seem to baffle Prime Minister David Cameron, who was caught off-guard vacationing in Italy. Even Chile is now on the protest map with violent student demonstrations. According to a CNN report,[86] in august of 2011, "More than 60,000 [students] demonstrators protested in Santiago."

Yemen, Libya, and many other countries are either on the list of countries where unrest has erupted, or are about to join it.

When you analyze the crises in each country, it is easy to see that social, economic, and political injustices are at the bottom of all of them. Yet, these wrongs are nothing new. They have plagued humankind for thousands of years. Why, then, is everyone protesting specifically now, and why is everyone protesting *simultaneously*?

The answers lie in the structure and evolution of human nature. As Jean M. Twenge and W. Keith Campbell beautifully illustrated in *The Narcissism Epidemic: Living in the Age of Entitlement* (Free Press, 2009), people today are not only narcissistic and self-centered, but are becoming more and more so at an alarming rate.

As narcissists, we put ourselves in the center of everything, and "grade" everyone else according to the benefits they may bring us. We connect to the world through the spectacles of self-entitlement. However, this is precisely how we *must not* function if we are to succeed in an era of globalization, when the world is interconnected and interdependent. To succeed, we must want to benefit those to whom we are connected just as much as we wish to benefit ourselves. If we are connected and dependent on each other, then if they are happy, so will we be. And if others are unhappy, we, too, will be unhappy, as demonstrated by Nicholas A. Christakis, MD, PhD, and James H. Fowler, PhD, in *Connected: The Surprising Power of Our Social Networks and How They Shape Our Lives – How Your Friends' Friends' Friends Affect Everything You Feel, Think, and Do.*

The solution, therefore, lies in shifting our viewpoint from self-entitlement to social-entitlement, putting our society first and our egos next, *in order to eventually benefit ourselves.*

In practical terms, this solution entails three goals:

1. Guaranteeing necessary provisions to every member of society.

2. Guaranteeing the continuation of those provisions by inculcating prosocial values into society using mass media and the internet, focusing on the social networks.

3. Using our prosocial work for self-enhancement so we can fully realize the potential that lies within each of us.

To achieve **Goal 1**, an international panel of statespersons, economists, and sociologists representing all the nations, must be set up to devise a plan to establish a just and sustainable economy. Note that the term "just" does not refer to equal distribution of funds or resources (natural or human). Rather, in a just economy no person on earth is left uncared for. Thus, a starving child in Kenya may not need the latest model of iPhone, but is undoubtedly entitled to proper nourishment, a roof over the head, proper education, and proper healthcare.

Conversely, a child of a similar age in Norway may already have the latest iPhone, but still feel miserable to the point of taking his or her own life, or worse yet, that of others, as recent events in that country have shown.[87] The distress in the two cases is very different but just as acute, and both must be addressed by the panel, keeping in mind that, as 2008 Nobel prize laureate and *The New*

York Times columnist, Paul Krugman, said, "We are all in the same boat."

Achieving **Goal 2** requires a shift of mindset. Since the media determines the public agenda, it is the media that must lead the way toward annihilating self-centeredness. Instead of the current "Me, me, me," attitude cultivated by the media over the past several decades, its new mottos should be "We, we, we," "mutual guarantee," and "one for all and all for one." If the media describes the benefits of mutual guarantee and the harm in the narcissistic approach, we will naturally gravitate toward sharing and caring, rather than toward suspecting and isolating ourselves. If commercials, infomercials, and infotainments begin to show veneration toward giving individuals, we will all begin to want to give, just as today when the media shows reverence to the rich and powerful, we want to be rich and powerful, as well.

Such a mindset will guarantee that our society remains just and compassionate toward all people, and at the same time that all the people *willingly* contribute to this society. Additionally, many of today's regulating and restraining agencies, such as the police, the army, and financial regulators will either become obsolete or require a fraction of the human and financial resources they currently require. Consequently, those resources will be directed toward improving our daily lives, rather than merely toward keeping them relatively safe, with diminishing success.

In such an encouraging and prosocial atmosphere, **Goal 3**, "Using our prosocial work for self-enhancement," will be a natural offshoot. Society will encourage, strive, and *make efforts* to guarantee that each of us realizes his or her personal potential to the maximum, because when that potential is used for the common good, society will benefit. Moreover, liberated from the need to protect ourselves from a hostile environment, a treasure trove of new energies will lend themselves to our self-realization. The result will be eradication of depression and all its related ills, and dramatically enhanced satisfaction from life.

After a few months of living in a society-oriented mindset, we will be baffled by how we could ever have thought that self-interest was a good idea. The evident success and happiness of such a society will yield ever growing motivation to promote and strengthen it, thus creating a perpetual motion in favor of society, and at the same time, in favor of each of its members without neglecting a single one of them.

In our globalized reality, only a form of government that deems the happiness and well-being of *all* the people in the world *equally important* can prove sustainable and successful.

THE ROAD TO
SOCIAL JUSTICE

Throughout the world, nations and peoples are awakening, demanding that their governments listen to them, recognize their pain, and resolve their problems. The uproar is not only over food or housing prices. At its base is a firm demand for *social justice*.

Yet, social justice is an elusive goal. With so many sections of society affected by inflation, unemployment, and a lack of education, one person's justice may very well lead to another person's injustice. In the current structure of society, whatever solution is reached, it will only perpetuate, if not exacerbate the current injustice, causing widespread disillusionment, which could trigger more violence or even war.

Thus, the solution to the demand for social justice must involve *all parts of society*, none excluded. The 2011 "Spring of the Nations" proves that the world has changed fundamentally. Humanity has become a single, global entity. As such, it requires that we acknowledge every part of it—both nations and individuals—as worthy in their own right. Nations no longer tolerate occupation, and people no longer tolerate oppression.

If we compare humanity to a human body containing numerous organs of different functions, no organ is redundant. Every organ both contributes what it should to the body, and receives what it needs.

Likewise, the approach to resolving the worldwide unrest must include *all* parts of society. The keywords to all negotiations involving government officials and protesters should be "thoughtful deliberation." The negotiations should be based on the premise that all parties' demands have merit and should be addressed respectfully. Yet, because so many parties have legitimate demands, all parties must take the other parties' demands into account, as well.

In such deliberations, there are no "good guys" or "bad guys." There are people with genuine, legitimate needs, sharing their problems with one another, trying to reach an acceptable, *dignified* solution for all.

Think of a large and loving family. Everyone in the family has his or her needs: Grandpa needs his pills, Dad needs a new suit for his new job, Mom needs her yoga lessons, and brother Ben has just been accepted into a high-priced college. So the family gets together for a family meeting, a bit like Thanksgiving but without the turkey. The members talk about incomes, argue over priorities, share their needs, squabble a bit, and laugh a lot. And in the end, they know what's necessary, what's not, who will get what he or she needs now, and who will get it later. But since they are family, connected by love, those who have to wait agree to wait because after all, they're family.

In many respects, globalization and growing interdependence have turned humanity into a giant-size family. Now we just need to learn how to work as such. If we think about it, a big family is always safer than being alone, provided it functions as a loving family.

Also, we must keep in mind that in almost every country, governments are struggling with mounting deficits and debt. There are not enough resources to go around, but there are certainly enough resources to allow respectable living for all, if only we *acknowledge* each other's needs. Therefore, the "big family way" is the best concept to ensure that social justice is eventually achieved. Just as in a family, the idea is not to break down the system, but to adjust it to cater to people's needs, rather than cater to the desires of various pressure groups.

King Arthur had a round table around which he and his knights would congregate. As its name suggests, the table had no head, implying that everyone who sat there was of equal status. Similarly, governments and citizens need to understand that there is no way to resolve social problems without sitting together at a round table (metaphorically if not physically).

We must remember that we are all mutually responsible for one another and that we are interdependent, like a family. The problems that seem to tackle us around each corner are not the causes, but the *symptoms* of our real problem: lack of solidarity and mutual responsibility for one another. Therefore, it is of utmost importance that we resolve them by calling in the "spirit of the round table."

By resolving these problems one at a time we will gradually build a society governed by mutual guarantee. Indeed, the mindset of mutual guarantee is the real reason we are presented with these problems. Once we achieve mutual guarantee, the problems will be gone like the wind.

TOWARD MUTUAL COMMITMENT

Why shared responsibility in facing the world's challenges is the key to resolving them in an interdependent world

Despite decades of unimaginable efforts, resources, and planning on the part of the UN to eradicate inequality, exploitation, and lack of basic conditions for sustaining life, these problems still pose major challenges in many countries. Around the world, some 1.4 billion people are living on less than $2 a day, while $5.2 billion worth of food are wasted every year in Australia alone.

Jonathan Bloom, author of *American Wasteland: How America Throws Away Nearly Half of Its Food*, writes that "More than 40 percent of the food produced for consumption is wasted by Americans. The total cost of food wasted comes out to an annual amount of more than $100 billion." Worse yet, the gap between those who have and those who have not continues to widen.

For decades, the efforts of developing nations to seek aid in food, health, and development from more affluent countries have been met with highly inadequate results. Until today there was no other choice. After all, the name of the game was "Winner Takes All."

The gaps are not only among countries, but also within them. The sense of deprivation causes both national and international tension, and clearly, given the global crisis, the situation can escalate drastically.

But now the game has changed. The recent emergence of the Spring of Nations is teaching all of us a lesson we should heed carefully: The world is connected, and what goes around comes around. Globalization has made us all interdependent, and no nation can exploit other nations simply because it is stronger, or it will pay dearly. As we can see, countries that yesterday seemed unassailable are crumbling today. They remain solvent only by the mercy of nations that, just a few years back, were treated as inferior.

In today's globalized reality, either we *all* win or we *all* lose, because we are interdependent. When enough people in the world open their eyes to the facts of globalization and shared responsibility, a major shift will begin. No longer will countries and peoples exploit one another; no longer will mammoth consortiums exploit tens of millions of underpaid workers around the world; no longer will children be allowed to die of hunger and illnesses that can be treated with common antibiotics, and no longer will women be abused simply because they are women. Indeed, in a world where people realize that their own well-being depends on the well-being of others, they will care for others, who will later care for them in return.

When that shift begins, terms such as "first world" and "third world" will cease to exist. There will be only one world and the people living in it.

CARRYING OUT THE SHIFT

To actualize the above-said, two things are of utmost importance: 1) first aid, 2) education.

By "first aid," we mean that we launch a worldwide campaign that explains why, in a globalized reality, insufficient food supply and lack of clean drinking water are inexcusable and must be corrected without delay. It is easy to show that the cost of such investments pays itself back with interest within a few short years. Countries such as India, Vietnam, and Indonesia serve as wonderful examples, despite all their still existing challenges.

Education means informing people of the new era of globalization, mutual dependence, and shared responsibility, of which we are all part. The recent global financial crises, and the series of uprisings around the world are sufficient evidence that we affect one another on all levels of life—economic, social, and even emotional (see Thomas Friedman's reference to "Globalization of Anger"[88]).

At **Stage One** of the education process, people will realize that it is unthinkable that over a billion people are starving while another billion is throwing away almost half the food it buys and struggles with obesity. Once the bare necessities of life have been provided to the entire world, Stage Two will begin.

Stage Two will focus on enhancing unity and solidarity among individuals and nations, in congruence with the current, interconnected reality.

In Nature, unity, reciprocity, and mutual responsibility are prerequisites to life. No organism survives unless its cells operate in harmony. Likewise, no ecosystem thrives if one of its elements is removed. Until recently, humanity was the only species that did not follow the law of mutual dependence and reciprocity. We believed that Nature's law was "Survival of the Fittest." But now we are beginning to realize that we, too, are subject to interdependence and must play by that rule if we are to survive.

The Campaign

To integrate the messages of mutual responsibility and interdependence, we suggest the following: to declare next year, which the U.N. titled, "The Year of Cooperatives," the starting point of shifting the global mindset toward the urgent need for mutual commitment in order to keep society and economy sustainable.

The Steps of the Shift

1) We should assemble an international forum of scientists (from hard sciences as well as social sciences and humanities), artists, thinkers, economists, successful businesspersons, and celebrities under the auspices of the U.N. to declare the start of the Year of Cooperatives. In that conference, the participants will commit to doing their utmost to eradicate hunger and deprivation. They will be chartered by their countries to devise a worldwide

campaign to instill the awareness of globalization, shared responsibility, and interdependence.

2) At the end of the forum, teams from the U.N. will work with each country to create media campaigns, school programs, street signs, and other means of advertisement to promote the abovementioned concepts. The goal of the campaign will be to make the idea of exploiting others abominable, and the idea of sharing and caring praiseworthy—and eventually, second nature for us all.

3) The U.N. teams will convene on a regular basis at U.N. headquarters to report on and synchronize their moves, thus promoting uniform global progress toward a sense of mutual responsibility. The teams' meetings will be broadcast live to demonstrate transparency and enhance their credibility. Most important will be the opportunity to show just how productive we can be when we work together.

4) Countries, consortiums, and even individuals who excel in demonstrating solidarity and shared responsibility will be praised and glorified, much the same as movie stars and pop stars are admired today. This will be a powerful incentive to encourage those who excel to continue excelling, and to those who are not, to join in.

5) From numerous experiments on the effects of prosocial behavior (such as David W. Johnson and Roger T. Johnson, "An Educational Psychology

Success Story: Social Interdependence Theory and Cooperative Learning"[89]), we know that typically Western afflictions such as depression and drug abuse will be all but gone when the campaign takes root. This, in turn, will free up a tremendous amount of financial and human resources to tend to humanity's other needs. International hostilities will also decrease tremendously, even if only for lack of moral and financial support of the adversaries. In an interdependent world, it is simply unwise to battle, and this will be very clear to all.

We at ARI Research have years of experience in international collaborations, networking, and circulation of ideas. We have an online system of free broadcasts simultaneously interpreted into eight languages, and we can produce text and video materials almost at a moment's notice.

We are already collaborating with UNESCO on the topic of global education, and we offer all our services and facilities gratis to the U.N. in hopes of expanding our fruitful partnership.

Today, Nature demands that we unite. Over time, that demand will intensify until we have all consented. At the same time, that demand is the key to our success in building a sustainable reality for ourselves and for our children. In light of all that, we must unite, work together, and we *will* succeed.

THE BENEFITS OF
THE NEW ECONOMY

A balanced economy is not only mandatory
in the global and integral reality,
it also benefits us all

Key Points

- An economy based on the principles of mutual guarantee is congruent with the laws of the global-integral system, and will therefore be stable and best provide for our reasonable needs of sustenance. It will also allow us to make time to realize our personal and social potentials.

- An economy under the umbrella of mutual guarantee has many social and economic advantages, such as a fair standard of living for all, reduction of the cost of living, transparency, a larger "economic pie," and a dramatic reduction of gaps and economic inequality.

- The transition from today's competitive, self-centered economy to a balanced, functional one will reveal many surpluses in money, assets, and resources that can be used for the public benefit.

- The transition to a mutual guarantee-based economy will be gradual, but from its inception a positive dynamic of change and hope will be created—a new spirit, a sense of cohesion and personal confidence.

AN ESCALATING CRISIS IN EUROPE
AND THE UNITED STATES

The global economic crisis is rapidly worsening. The United States suffered its first ever downgrade of its credit rating, and the Eurozone is threatening to collapse altogether, or alternately, face insolvency of sovereign debt, which would shake up financial markets all over the world. At the same time, leading economists are making foreboding statements, such as Nouriel Roubini's, "There's a significant probability ... that over the next 12 months, there's going to be another recession in most advanced economies,"[90] or Joseph E. Stiglitz's, "In a way, not only there is a crisis in our economy, there ought to be a crisis in economics."[91]

The economic interdependence among countries makes it impossible for them to isolate themselves and resolve their problems separately. An example of that is the attempt of the Eurozone to save the faltering Greek economy. The Polish Finance Minister, Jacek Rostowski, speaking before the European Parliament, warned that "Europe is in danger, and the breakdown of the Eurozone would lead to a chain reaction leading to the breakup of the European Union (EU) and ultimately to the return of war in Europe."[92] Also, German Chancellor Angela Merkel stated that "Euro-region leaders must erect a firewall around Greece to avert a cascade of market attacks on other European states."[93]

Naturally, investors are concerned about the future of the world economy. During weekend talks of policy makers, investors and bankers in Washington, PIMCO, the world's largest bond investor, predicted, "Economies will stall over the next year as Europe slides into a recession."[94]

Regarding that same event, former U.S. Treasury Secretary, Lawrence Summers, said he has been to 20 years of International Monetary Fund (IMF) gatherings, and "There's not been a prior meeting at which matters have had more gravity, and at which I've been more concerned about the future of the global economy."

Unemployment in Europe and the United States is high and rising. For example, Spain's unemployment rate rose sharply to a new Eurozone high of 21.3 percent in the first quarter of the year, with a record 4.9 million people out of work.[95] In the United States, the unemployment rate is 8.6, with 13.3 million people out of work.[96]

THE ECONOMY NEEDS A MAKEOVER

The failure to resolve the global crisis that began in 2008 baffles the most prominent economists and exposes the limitations of the current economic paradigms. The expansive monetary policy was meant to reverse the decline and gradually heal the world economy, but the reverse seems to have happened. It appears that the economic "toolbox" in the hands of decision-makers treated only the symptoms of the crisis rather than the crisis itself.

The interest rate cuts, expansion of budgets—intended to boost industry and commerce—tax cuts, reforms in finance, interference of central banks in bond and currency markets have all failed to reinvigorate the stalled economy.

To resolve the crisis, we must first diagnose the root of the problem and adopt a solution that corrects it. Treating only the symptoms doesn't resolve the crisis itself, as its recent re-emergence indicates.

At its very heart, the economy is an expression of how we relate to each other. In the current economy, our primary motive is to maximize our profits in a competitive environment that perpetuates in us the sense of lack. This results in a zero-sum-game, where one's gain comes at the expense of another.

The solution to the economic crisis requires us to first change our relationships into those based on mutual guarantee. Such a change will be possible only by creating a supportive environment, including information systems that educate us about this change. These will include use of the media, as well as adult and youth education systems. The educational framework will endorse such values as solidarity, collaboration, empathy, care for others, and mutual guarantee.

Social sciences provide ample proof of how the environment influences people.[97] Hence, we must build a society that teaches us to think differently and to adopt prosocial values.

Today, society rewards us with money, power, and glory. Such rewards create competition and induce aggressiveness as each of us tries to exploit or manipulate others on personal, company, national, or international levels. If the rewards were to change and, instead, encouraged mutual guarantee, the change would be easy to make and would have broad public support. This is the power of the environment to influence our behavior.

FIRST THINGS FIRST: PUTTING OUT THE FIRE

First, we must put out the fires and deal with the most pressing issues facing us. To do so, we must come together, deliberate in a round-table format, and discuss—just like a family—how we can help those among us who are in desperate need, living below the poverty line. Without a solution for such problems that we can all agree on, we cannot make any progress.

Agreement is a precondition of forming the mutual guarantee among us. Agreeing on mutual guarantee will enable the more fortunate to make the necessary concessions to assist others and create the economic amendments that will thoroughly deal with the challenges of poverty.

Some of the financing to mend the imbalance will come from state budgets, reflecting the change in socioeconomic priorities. However, the bulk of the money will come from new sources created by the transition from excessive consumerism to reasonable consumption. That transition will reflect the change from an individualistic, competitive economy to a collaborative, harmonious one that is in sync with the laws of the global, integral world.

At the same time, we must acquire basic life skills and initiate consumer education to qualify us to pursue an independent, balanced way of living in the new world. Combining immediate economic and financial solutions with proper consumer education will act as "CPR" for the lower-income individuals in society. It will also forge the common basis necessary to adopt mutual guarantee as a social and economic treaty, tying us all together, in sync with the laws of the global-integral world.

TOWARD A NEW ECONOMY, UNDER THE UMBRELLA OF MUTUAL GUARANTEE

It is easy to describe the improved socioeconomic system at the end of the transformation process, towards which this crisis is drawing us. The inadequacy of the current economic systems in the global network and the increasing personal and political interdependence are the real reasons for the escalating global crisis. When decision-makers and leading economists grasp that these are the core issues, the solution will become obvious, though we will still need to change our relations to those of mutual guarantee. Once accomplished, we can move to a new economy that reflects this shift of ideas and values in the world.

Under the umbrella of mutual guarantee, both the economy and human society will be in harmony with the global network of connections. Instead of "sailing against the wind," wasting energy and resources trying to maintain a failing economic method, a new economy will form, both balanced and stable, relying on solid social cohesion on all levels, expansive international cooperation, balanced consumption, and stable financial markets. This will be a far cry from the current financial markets, which produce destructive bubbles every 5-7 years.

BENEFITS OF THE ECONOMY OF MUTUAL GUARANTEE

There are many benefits to an economy based on mutual guarantee. By attempting to cling to the existing, failing economic model and ease the immediate problems following the financial crisis, we are making it harder to appreciate the vast potential of the mutual guarantee economy. If we imagine that we are already in a state of mutual guarantee, we will be able to see its many advantages:

1) **A just and fair standard of living for all:** An economic policy based on mutual consideration will help us allocate the necessary public funds to raise the lower classes above the poverty line. At the same time, workshops, life skills training and consumer science will help people develop financial independence. Living beyond our means and over-consumption have become a global liability that requires correction..[98,99]

2) **Lowering the cost of living:** When greed is no longer the basis of our economic relations, when each of us is content with a reasonable profit and

does not aspire to maximize profit at the expense of others, the prices of products and services will drop to near-production cost. Today, the prices of many goods and services are too high because each link along the commercial chain strives to achieve maximum benefit. Extolling the value of mutual guarantee in communication networks and in the public discourse will make firms add public benefit to their equations. This will make life more affordable for all of us.

The first signs of a cost-lowering movement are already emerging. Social unrest is actually causing manufacturers to lower the prices of products and services. For now, these are variable, occasional, minor, and passing discounts, but the trend is clear. When we transition to a relatively balanced consumption pattern, both demand and prices will be come down.

Also, diminishing the cost of living will diminish inequality and social gaps, one of the primary advantages of the mutual guarantee economy.

3) **Diminishing social gaps:** One of the primary ills of the present global economy is a constant increase in inequality. This is the prime initiator of the worldwide unrest that demands social justice. When we treat each other like family, we will not tolerate inequality of opportunity or means among us or anywhere in the world. Instead of unrest and fear of revolution and violence, the mutual

guarantee economy will yield broad consent as economic gaps are diminished, and the stability of the system is enhanced.

Diminishing inequality means, among other things, economic and social concessions on the part of the top income earners. Education, the influence of the environment, and an effective mechanism of communication—such as the round table—will make certain that all decisions are reached with transparency and fairness, and reflect the social and economic consensus—imperative for mutual guarantee. In return for their concessions for the common good, those who make them will be rewarded with public appreciation for their contributions. Additionally, those who receive assistance and resources will be able to enjoy a better, more dignified life. They, too, will appreciate the new method.

4) **A genuine, thorough budget reform:** The only thing that can create a sense of social justice and mutual guarantee for each individual in society is the belief that we are all in the same boat, and must work together. This will require a fairer method of prioritizing in the national budget, reached by broad consensus, not through the squabbles of lobbyists and pressure groups.

An economy managed with transparency will allow everyone to understand how decisions are made, and will even help people influence them. When we feel a sense of partnership and involvement, we no longer feel negative emotions such as the frustration that currently exists toward policy makers. This lessening of negativity will allow people to agree with and support the decisions made by decision-makers, even when some of their choices are not popular. The satisfaction of acting as one family that makes decisions at the round table will encourage us to make concessions to each other.

5) **Increasing the financial "pie":** If every citizen, business, and government office feels part of the global family, many extras will appear in money, goods and services, state and municipal budgets, and even in our personal budgets. Consider how many things we have at home that we never use. We can take our surplus food and clothing, give it to the poor, and put the financial extras toward covering a significant portion of others' current needs. This will not even require an increase in the budget deficit, or impose austerity means or taxes.

However, we are not suggesting charity as a solution, although charity is a great expression of a solid community life and mutual assistance. Rather, we are talking about efficacy. For example, according to a CNN report, 30% of all food produced in the world each year is wasted or lost. That's about 1.3 billion tons, according to a report by the U.N. Food and Agriculture Organization.[100]

Why can't countries where hunger is a real problem receive that surplus? The answer, in a word, is "interests." Distributing the surplus food means increasing the supply, which would lead to lower prices. This, in turn, would diminish the profits of food producers and marketers. In an economy based on mutual guarantee, such a situation would be impossible. How can we throw away food when members of our family are starving?

This is just one example. For more examples of the benefits of mutual guarantee economy, see chapter, "Surplus and Improving Public Well-Being," in *The Benefits of the New Economy*.

6) **Improving employer-employee relations and firm-government relations:** Research in behavioral psychology indicates that wealthy people seek respect, not money.[101] Yet, today companies and CEOs are evaluated based on their profits and gains. Greater profit means a higher ranking in rating firms or appearance on the list of "most successful CEOs of the year."

Possibly the best example of this narrow, self-centered thinking of maximizing profits is the U.S. job market. The reason why the American job market is not adding more jobs, even as the economy grows, is that firms prefer to increase their workers' overtime, or shift part-time workers into working full time, rather than hire new people.

Today, such considerations are considered logical. But in an economy conducted by mutual guarantee, the values will be such that more people will be able to share in the prosperity of the economy, rather than fewer people sharing more of the profits. Similar improvements will be made in companies' relations with the government and tax authorities, leading to fairer taxes and fewer tax evasions.

7) **Stability and long-term solutions:** The new economy will be based on the values of mutual guarantee, and will necessarily be consistent with today's global interdependence. Such an economic method, in harmony and balance with the global and integral network, will be more stable and sustainable than all the existing economic and social methods. It would match its environment and reflect a broad consensus among its elements: people, companies, and states. A balanced economy that is friendly toward both man and Nature would allow each person to live in dignity, to feel that the system was personally "friendly," and to receive sufficient sustenance, along with the opportunity to reciprocate by contributing to the system.

8) **Certainty:** The transition to the new economy will be gradual. At first, there will be dynamics of change and hope, a new spirit in society, a sense of cohesion and personal security. The current fear of

being exploited will make way for concessions and gestures of generosity in several areas, such as more affordable housing prices, employment contracts that do not exploit workers, a simpler bureaucracy that truly serves the public interest, fair banks, and service providers that actually provide the intended service at a sane price. In short, people will feel confident in their interrelations, a feeling so badly needed in these uncertain times, and one that money truly cannot buy.

9) **True happiness:** The new economy will create in us a sense of fulfillment that cannot be measured with money. As described in *Benefits of the New Economy*, chapter, "Studies Challenge the Notion that Money Means Happiness," beyond a certain level of income, additional money does not improve one's feeling. Instead, people get satisfaction from successful relationships, from a sense of confidence and self-fulfillment. The new economy and its benefits are not transient, but are solid and stable because they are in sync with the laws of mutual guarantee. These enable a decision-making process based on a broad consensus.

10) **An applicable decision-making process:** As the new economy will be conducted with transparency, everyone will see how decisions are made and will be able to influence them. This is the only way to establish a practical decision-making process that will make people feel that decisions are both fair and

unbiased, reached after thorough consideration of *everyone's* needs. This will also enhance the stability of the socio-economic system.

11) **Economic and financial stability:** Money markets have changed from a meeting ground for companies and investors into a battleground of aggressive global players, with enough power to rattle and shake global market in pursuit of "an extra buck," regardless of the soundness of the system. A mutual guarantee economy will allow money markets to avoid repeatedly falling into financial bubbles that pop and lead to disaster in the real economy.

12) **Balanced consumption:** The pursuit of excessive consumption has long become a key element in our lives and in the world economy. In the mutual guarantee economy, this will gradually make way for balanced consumption. In fact, the process has already begun, thanks to the present crisis and the gradual transition from a competitive, wasteful, and unequal economy to a balanced, functional one whose goal is to provide for everyone's basic needs. Commercials and other forms of social pressure to convince us to buy redundant products and services will disappear, as will numerous superfluous brands and products. Instead, the desire to contribute to society and participate in community life for the common good will replace them as one's pride and joy.

Also, because of the decreased demand, prices will drop and reasonable, dignified living will become affordable to all. Companies will produce only what is truly necessary for us to lead a comfortable and balanced life.

13) **Global balance and harmony:** The transition from excessive consumption to balanced buying will reveal that Earth contains sufficient resources to sustain all of us comfortably for many years to come. The exploitation of natural resources will stop, and we will discover Earth's magnificent rejuvenation abilities.

The stability of the mutual guarantee economy is based on strong social cohesion and mutual concern. That stability requires that we understand that in an era of globalization, our interdependence requires us to adapt our connections and our social and economic systems into a single, harmonious system. It will provide for the needs of all of humanity, and support and encourage everyone's needs to realize the great potential within them.

THE MUTUAL GUARANTEE –
EDUCATIONAL AGENDA

Education is a recognized problem and a painful issue the world over. Uninterested children, declining grades, violence, and disorderly conduct indicate that the education systems in many countries have become dysfunctional.

Some of the problems originate in the structure of the education system and in its inability to adapt to changes. Yet, a change is clearly necessary, particularly because little has changed in schools since their inception back in the days of the Industrial Revolution some 200 years ago. Crowded classrooms, children behind desks, forced to sit still for extended periods of time, short breaks, and vast amounts of useless information to be memorized are still the norm. In the days when schools were first established, there was a genuine need to educate masses of workers to fill the assembly lines.

Thus, the current structure of schools reflects a very narrow perspective of the concept of education. The *Encyclopedia Britannica*, however, defines education in the following way: "Education can be thought of as the transmission of the values and accumulated knowledge of a society. In this sense, it is equivalent to what social scientists term socialization or enculturation. Children— whether conceived among New Guinea tribespeople, the Renaissance Florentines, or the middle classes of Manhattan—are born without culture. Education is designed to guide them in learning a culture, molding their behavior in the ways of adulthood, and directing them toward their eventual role in society."[102]

Yet, schools today merely aim to equip students with tools by which to continue their schooling at universities and colleges. Schools *do not* educate in the full sense of the word.

Education, as has just been described, is not merely the act of providing knowledge. It is a process for designing the personality and behavior of each of us. Indeed, the essence of education is to teach the student how to cope with and succeed in life. A school that teaches merely how to memorize information is irrelevant in today's reality.

In light of all the above, we have come to realize that we need to make a fundamental change in the educational paradigm. We must examine the challenges that the modern world presents to us and see whether the education we currently provide addresses them sufficiently.

In today's reality, our world has become a global village socially, politically, and economically. From the moment we became attached to one another, we lost the ability to continue leading our lives by values of narcissism and disregard for others. These values may have been useful in the old, individual, and egocentric world, but from the moment humanity turned into an integral, global system, the rules have become identical to those that apply to all integral systems in Nature.

The human body is an example of such an integral system. Within our bodies, the cooperation and harmony (known as homeostasis) among all cells and organs enable the body to maintain proper health. To remain healthy, each cell and organ operates according to the interests of the entire organism. The harmony among the cells turns the healthy body into the astounding machine that it is, and the health of the body contributes, in turn, to the health of each individual cell.

The way the cells in our bodies operate manifests the law of mutual guarantee and reciprocity, which applies to all multilateral connections in Nature. Indeed, the sustainability of the system depends on the reciprocal relations among the elements that comprise it.

Therefore, as long as we continue to relate to one another egoistically, in contrast to the world that has become integral, we act in dissonance with the laws of Nature. In doing so, we are like cells that are parts of an organism, yet consume only for themselves. In the case of the human body, the result of such cells is a cancerous tumor. In the case of humanity, the result is a multilayered, multifaceted global crisis.

To resolve this crisis, we must adjust our network of connections and make it truly global. Each person must recognize the nature of the world we live in, and understand that in the 21st century, one's personal life depends on one's attitude toward others. Therefore, we must educate people to become sensitive toward others, caring, and responsible in their approach to the world.

It follows that in the 21st century, the world needs more than an economic or political solution to its problems. First and foremost, it needs an educational solution.

Numerous studies and books have already determined that the paramount element in the molding of a young person's personality is the surrounding environment.[103] Therefore, to truly "educate" a child means to place him or her in the right environment, one that affects positive results and the right values. To bring up a generation that will annihilate the crises the world is currently experiencing, we must create a different social environment for our children.

From early on, children need to grow up with the understanding that egoism, the desire to enjoy at the expense of others, is the primary cause of suffering in the adult world. At the same time, we must show children—using various teaching aids—that relationships based on mutual consideration, tolerance, and understanding facilitate harmony and the persistence of life.

TEN KEY PRINCIPLES FOR GLOBAL EDUCATION

1) **The social environment builds the person:** The social environment is the principal element affecting children. Therefore, we must create among them a "miniature society" where everyone cares for everyone else. A child who grows up in such an environment will not only thrive and

succeed in expressing his or her creative potential, but will also approach life with a sense of purpose, and with a desire to build a similar society in the "exo-school" environment.

2) **Personal example:** Children learn from the examples we provide them, both personally—from educators and parents—and through the media and other public contents to which they are exposed.

3) **Equality:** During the learning process, there should not be a teacher, but an educator. Although the educator is older in age, he or she will be perceived by the children as "one of them," a peer. In this way, the educator can gradually "pull up" the children in every aspect of the study—informational, as well as moral and social. Thus, for example, during class, children and educators will sit in a circle and talk, with everyone treated as equals.

4) **Teaching through games:** Through games, children grow, learn, and deepen their understanding of how things are connected. A game is a means by which children get to know the world. In fact, children do not learn words by hearing them. Rather, they learn through *experience*. Therefore, it is necessary to use games as a primary method in working with children. The games should be built in such a way that children will see that they cannot succeed alone, but only with the help of others, that to succeed they must make concessions

to others, and that a good social environment can only do them good.

5) **Weekly outings:** Every week there should be a day when the children leave the school and go to a place in the country or some other location, depending on the child's age. Such places can be parks, zoos, factories, farms, movie studios, or theatres. Also, children should be taught how the systems that affect our lives operate, such as the law enforcement, the post office, hospitals, government offices, old-age homes, and any place where children can learn about the processes that are a part of our lives. Before, during, and following the outing, discussions should be held regarding what will be seen, how the experience compared with their expectations, their conclusions, and so forth.

6) **Older teaching the younger:** The older age groups will "adopt" younger groups, while the younger groups will tutor those who are younger still. In this way, everyone feels part of the learning process and acquires necessary tools for communicating with others.

7) **"Little court":** As part of the learning process, children should act out situations that they encounter in their daily lives: envy, power struggles, deceit, and so on. After acting them out, they should try to scrutinize them.

Through such experiences, children will learn to understand and be sensitive to others. They will comprehend that others can be in the right, too, even if they cannot accept their views at the moment. They will see that tomorrow they might find themselves in a similar situation, that every person and every view has its place in the world, and that everyone should be treated with tolerance.

8) **Video taping activities:** It is recommended that all activities be videotaped for later viewing and analysis together with the children. In this way, children will be able to see how they reacted or behaved in certain situations. They will be able to analyze the changes they are going through and develop the ability to introspect.

9) **Small groups with several educators:** It is highly recommended that each group of 10 students has a team of two educators and a supporting professional (a psychologist).

10) **Parent support:** The parents must support the educational process unfolding at school. They should talk to the children about the importance of the values inculcated at school, set a personal example of these values in their behavior, and completely avoid instilling other values. To facilitate this, there should also be courses for parents.

COLLABORATION WITH UNESCO

The method of global education has been warmly accepted by the Director-General of UNESCO, Mrs. Irina Bokova. At the moment, a UNESCO-ARI joint book on global education is in the making, and a series of international conferences and meetings has taken place and is planned for the future.

NOTES

1   An Address to the 2011 International Finance Forum by Christine Lagarde, Managing Director, International Monetary Fund, Beijing, November 9, 2011 (http://www.imf.org/external/np/speeches/2011/110911.htm)

2   Gordon Brown speaks to the Lord Mayor's Banquet: http://www.labour.org.uk/lord_mayors_banquet

3   D'Vera Cohn, Jeffrey Passel, Wendy Wang and Gretchen Livingston, "Barely Half of U.S. Adults Are Married – A Record Low," *Pew Research Center* (December 14, 2011), http://www.pewsocialtrends.org/2011/12/14/barely-half-of-u-s-adults-are-married-a-record-low/?src=prc-headline

4   "National survey shows a rise in illicit drug use from 2008 to 2010," *SAMHSA News Release* (August 9, 2011), http://www.samhsa.gov/newsroom/advisories/1109075503.aspx

5   Albert R. Hunt, "A Country of Inmates," *The New York Times* (November 20, 2011), http://www.nytimes.com/2011/11/21/us/21iht-letter21.html?pagewanted=all

6   Nicholas D. Kristof, "Our Broken Escalator," *The New York Times* (July 16, 2011), http://www.nytimes.com/2011/07/17/opinion/sunday/17kristof.html?_r=2

7   Richard Vedder and Matthew Denhart, "Why does college cost so much?" *CNN* (December 2, 2011), http://edition.cnn.com/2011/12/02/opinion/vedder-college-costs/index.html

8   National Rifle Association Institute for Legislative Action, "Firearm Fact Card 2011," http://www.nraila.org/Issues/FactSheets/Read.aspx?ID=83

9   Carol Cratty, "Gun sales at record levels, according to FBI background checks," *CNN* (December 28, 2011), http://edition.cnn.com/2011/12/27/us/record-gun-sales/index.html

10   Kate Kelland, "Nearly 40 Percent of Europeans Suffer Mental Illness," *Reuters* (September 4, 2011), http://www.reuters.com/article/2011/09/04/us-europe-mental-illness-idUSTRE7832JJ20110904

11   Toby Helm, "Most Britons believe children will have worse lives than their parents – poll," *The Guardian* (December 3, 2011), http://www.guardian.co.uk/society/2011/dec/03/britons-children-lives-parents-poll

12   Scott Hamilton, "Roubini: Slowdown Brings Forward New Crisis," *Bloomberg* (September 6, 2011), http://www.bloomberg.com/news/2011-09-06/roubini-says-global-economic-slowdown-accelerating-next-financial-crisis.html

140   A Guide to the New World

13   Michael Babad, "George Soros: 'We are on the verge of an economic collapse,'" *The Globe and Mail* (June 27, 2011), http://www.theglobeandmail.com/report-on-business/top-business-stories/george-soros-we-are-on-the-verge-of-an-economic-collapse/article2076789/

14   James Kirkup, "World facing worst financial crisis in history, Bank of England Governor says," *The Telegraph* (October 6, 2011), http://www.telegraph.co.uk/finance/financialcrisis/8812260/World-facing-worst-financial-crisis-in-history-Bank-of-England-Governor-says.html

15   Ian Goldin, "Navigating our global future," *TED* (October 2009), http://www.ted.com/talks/ian_goldin_navigating_our_global_future.html

16   Fareed Zakaria, "Get Out the Wallets: The world needs Americans to spend, *Newsweek* (August 1, 2009), http://www.newsweek.com/2009/07/31/get-out-the-wallets.html

17   "U.S. Debt Reaches 100 Percent of Country's GDP," *Fox News* (August 4, 2011), http://www.foxnews.com/politics/2011/08/04/us-debt-reaches-100-percent-countrys-gdp/#ixzz1jlhe6Qly

18   "The Debt to the Penny and Who Holds It," *Treasury Direct*, http://www.treasurydirect.gov/NP/NPGateway

19   Tim Jackson, "Tim Jackson's economic reality check" *TED* (October 2010), http://www.ted.com/talks/lang/en/tim_jackson_s_economic_reality_check.html (min. 06:59)

20   Anthony Giddens, *Runaway World: How Globalization is Reshaping Our Lives* (N.Y., Routledge, 2003), 6-7.

21   Javier Solana and Daniel Innerarity, "The New Grammar of Power," *Project Syndicate* (July 1, 2011), http://www.project-syndicate.org/commentary/solana10/English)

22   Ludger Kühnhardt "A Call for the United States to Rediscover Its Ideals," *The Globalist* (May 24, 2011), http://www.theglobalist.com/storyid.aspx?StoryId=9149

23   Pascal Lamy "Lamy underlines need for 'unity in our global diversity,'" *World Trade Organization* (WTO) (June 14, 2011), http://www.wto.org/english/news_e/sppl_e/sppl194_e.htm

24   Gregory Rodriguez, "Rodriguez: Zero-sum games in an interconnected world," *Los Angeles Times* (August 1, 2011), http://articles.latimes.com/2011/aug/01/opinion/la-oe-rodriguez-zero-sum-20110801

25   L'Oeil de La Lettre, "'Think We, Not Me or I'–The Dalai Lama," *La Lettre*, http://www.lalettredelaphotographie.com/entries/think-we-not-me-or-i-the-dalai-lama

26   Alice Calaprice, *The New Quotable Einstein* (USA: Princeton University Press, 2005), 206

27   Information extracted from the MIT Haystack Observatory, www.haystack.mit.edu/edu/pcr/.../3%20.../nuclear%20synthesis.pdf.

28   Werner Heisenberg, quoted by Ruth Nanda Anshen in *Biography of an Idea* (Moyer Bell, 1987), 224

29   G. Tyler Miller, Scott Spoolman, *Living in the Environment: Principles, Connections, and Solutions*, 16th Edition (U.S.A., Brooks/Cole, September 24, 2008), 15

30   Jean M. Twenge and W. Keith Campbell, *The Narcissism Epidemic: Living in the Age of Entitlement* (New York: Free Press, A Division of Simon & Schuster, Inc. 2009), 78

31   Jean M. Twenge and W. Keith Campbell, *The Narcissism Epidemic*, 1

32   Jean M. Twenge and W. Keith Campbell, *The Narcissism Epidemic*, 1-2

33   Fiona Harvey, "World headed for irreversible climate change in five years, IEA warns," *The Guardian* (November 9, 2011), http://www.guardian.co.uk/environment/2011/nov/09/fossil-fuel-infrastructure-climate-change

34   e360 digest, "Extreme Weather Events Likely Linked to Warming, IPCC Says" (November 1, 2011), http://e360.yale.edu/digest/extreme_weather_events_likely_linked_to_warming_ipcc_says/3195/

35   "Fishing, Why It Matters, *WWF*, http://www.worldwildlife.org/what/globalmarkets/fishing/whyitmatters.html

36   Ian Sample, "Global food crisis looms as climate change and population growth strip fertile land" (*The Guardian*, August 31, 2007), http://www.guardian.co.uk/environment/2007/aug/31/climatechange.food

37   "Water, Sanitation and Hygiene," *UNICEF* (December 21, 2011), http://www.unicef.org/wash/

38   Lester R. Brown, *World on the Edge: How to Prevent Environmental and Economic Collapse* (USA, W. W. Norton & Company, January 6, 2011), 16

39   Matthew Lee, "Hillary Clinton Raises Alarm on Rising Food Prices," *Associated Press* (May 6, 2011), published on cnsnews.com, http://cnsnews.com/news/article/hillary-clinton-raises-alarm-rising-food-prices

40   Ramy Inocencio, "World wastes 30% of all food," *CNN* (May 13, 2011), http://business.blogs.cnn.com/2011/05/13/30-of-all-worlds-food-goes-to-waste/

41   "Ethics And The Global Financial Crisis," interview with Michel Camdessus, uploaded to YouTube by romereports (April 1, 2009), http://www.youtube.com/watch?v=M3q8XFLDWlg

42   Steve Connor, "Warning: Oil supplies are running out fast," *The Independent* (August 3, 2009), http://www.independent.co.uk/news/science/warning-oil-supplies-are-running-out-fast-1766585.html

43   Quoted in: Laszlo Solymar, Donald Walsh, *Lectures on the electrical properties of materials*, "Introduction" (UK, Oxford University Press, 1993), xiii

44   Martin Luther King, Jr. "Facing the Challenge of a New Age" (December, 1956), http://www.libertynet.org/edcivic/king.html

45   Nicholas A. Christakis, *James H. Fowler, Connected: The Surprising Power of Our Social Networks and How They Shape Our Lives -- How Your Friends' Friends' Friends Affect Everything You Feel, Think, and Do* (USA, Little, Brown and Company, January 12, 2011), 305

46   Maria Konnikova, "Lessons from Sherlock Holmes: The Power of Public Opinion," *Scientific American*, "Blogs" (September 13, 2011), http://blogs.scientificamerican.com/guest-blog/2011/09/13/lessons-from-sherlock-holmes-the-power-of-public-opinion/

47   Kavita Abraham Dowsing, PhD, and James Deane, "The Power of Public Discourse," http://wbi.worldbank.org/wbi/devoutreach/article/1298/power-public-discourse

48   Source: Saul Mcleod, "Asch Experiment," *Simply Psychology*, 2008, http://www.simplypsychology.org/asch-conformity.html

49   "Thanks for the Memories," an experiment in false memories conducted by Prof. Yadin Dudai and Micah Edelson of the Institute's Neurobiology Department, together with Prof. Raymond Dolan and Dr. Tali Sharot of University College London (released August 29, 2011), http://wis-wander.weizmann.ac.il/thanks-for-the-memories

50   Erich Fromm, *The Art of Loving* (U.S.A., Harper Perennial, September 5, 2000), 13

51   Eryn Brown, "Violent video games and changes in the brain," *Los Angeles Times* (November 30, 2011), http://www.latimes.com/health/boostershots/la-heb-violent-videogame-brain-20111130,0,6877853.story

52   Following the July 22, 2011 attack on Norwegians by a Norway native: "Report: Norwegian Retailer Pulls Violent Games In Wake Of Attack," *DigiPen Institute of Technology* (July 29, 2011), http://www.gamecareerguide.com/industry_news/36185/report_norwegian_retailer_pulls_.php

53 David Jenkins, "Mass Shooting In Germany Prompts Retailer To Drop Mature-Rated Games," *Gamasutra* (March 20, 2009), http://www.gamasutra.com/news/production/?story=22839

54 University of Michigan Health System, "Television and Children," http://www.med.umich.edu/yourchild/topics/tv.htm

55 Martin Buber, philosopher and educator, *A Nation and a World: Essays on current events*, trans. from Hebrew: Chaim Ratz (Israel, Zionistic Library Publications, 1964), 220

56 George Monbiot, "The British boarding school remains a bastion of cruelty," *The Guardian* (January 16, 2012), http://www.guardian.co.uk/commentisfree/2012/jan/16/boarding-school-bastion-cruelty. Note: While this story addresses the problems of schools in the U.K., the data it gives of the state of Texas schools is no less alarming.

57 Victoria Burnett, "A Job and No Mortgage for All in a Spanish Town," *The New York Times* (May 25, 2009), http://www.nytimes.com/2009/05/26/world/europe/26spain.html?pagewanted=all

58 Andy Sernovitz, *Word of Mouth Marketing: How Smart Companies Get People Talking, Revised Edition*, (U.S.A. Kaplan Press, February 3, 2009), 4

59 Clive Thompson, "Are Your Friends Making You Fat?", *The New York Times* (September 10, 2009), http://www.nytimes.com/2009/09/13/magazine/13contagion-t.html?_r=1&th&emc=th

60 (ibid.)
61 (ibid.)
62 (ibid.)

63 "Nicholas Christakis: The hidden influence of social networks" (a talk, quote taken from minute 17:11), TED 2010, http://www.ted.com/talks/nicholas_christakis_the_hidden_influence_of_social_networks.html

64 "ILO warns of major G20 labour market decline in 2012 and serious jobs shortfall by 2015," *International Labor Organization* (ILO) (September 26, 2011), http://www.ilo.org/global/about-the-ilo/press-and-media-centre/news/WCMS_163835/lang--en/index.htm

65 Daniel Woolls, "Spain's Unemployment Rate Hits New Eurozone Record Of 21.3 Percent," *The Huffington Post* (April 29, 2011), http://www.huffingtonpost.com/2011/04/29/span-unemployment-inflation-economy-debt_n_855341.html

66 "Employment Situation Summary," *Bureau of Labor Statistics* (January 6, 2012), www.bls.gov/news.release/empsit.nr0.htm

67 Felix Salmon, "The global youth unemployment crisis," *Reuters* (December 22, 2011), http://blogs.reuters.com/felix-salmon/2011/12/22/the-global-youth-unemployment-crisis/

68   Ulrich Beck, *The Brave New World of Work* (USA, Polity, 1 edition, January 15, 2000), 2

69   Thomas L. Friedman, "The Earth is Full," *The New York Times* (June 7, 2011), http://www.nytimes.com/2011/06/08/opinion/08friedman. html?scp=1&sq=the%20earth%20is%20full%20thomas%20 friedman&st=cse

70   Adir Cohen, *The gate of light: Janusz Korczak, the educator and writer who overcame the Holocaust* (USA, Fairleigh Dickinson Univ Press, Dec 1, 1994), 31

71   David W. Johnson and Roger T. Johnson, "An Educational Psychology Success Story: Social Interdependence Theory and Cooperative Learning," *Educational Researcher* 38 (2009): 365, doi: 10.3102/0013189X09339057

72   Johnson and Johnson, "Educational Psychology Success Story," 368

73   Johnson and Johnson, "Educational Psychology Success Story," 371

74   (ibid.)

75   For more on education, see Appendix 1: The Mutual Guarantee–Educational Agenda

76   Christine Lagarde, "The Path Forward—Act Now and Act Together," *International Monetary Fund* (IMF) (September 23, 2011), http://www.imf.org/external/np/speeches/2011/092311.htm

77   "Minority Rules: Scientists Discover Tipping Point for the Spread of Ideas," *SCNARC* (July 26, 2011), http://scnarc.rpi.edu/content/minority-rules-scientists-discover-tipping-point-spread-ideas

78   Appears in "The Oneness of Mind," as translated in *Quantum Questions: Mystical Writings of the World's Great Physicists*, edited by Ken Wilber (USA, Shambhala Publications, Inc., Revised edition, April 10, 2001), 87

79   Mohamed A. El-Erian, "The Anatomy of Global Economic Uncertainty," *Project Syndicate* (November 18, 2011), http://www.project-syndicate.org/commentary/elerian11/English

80   Albert Einstein, Alice Calaprice and Freeman Dyson, *The Ultimate Quotable Einstein* (USA, Princeton University Press, October 11, 2010), 476

81   Efrat Peretz, "We Must Prepare for a World of Equal Revenue Sharing," trans. Chaim Ratz, *Globes* (October 18, 2011), http://www. globes.co.il/news/article.aspx?QUID=1057,U1319062129813&d id=1000691044

82   Dr. Joseph E. Stiglitz, "Imagining an Economics that Works: Crisis, Contagion and the Need for a New Paradigm," *The New Palgrave Dictionary of Economics Online* (min 1:36), http://www.dictionaryofeconomics.com/resources/news_lindau_meeting

83   "Fischer on Fed's Toolbox," CNBC Video (August 25, 2011), http://video.cnbc.com/gallery/?video=3000041703#eyJ2aWQiOiIzMD-AwMDQxNzAzIiwiZW5jVmlkIjoiZ2FJT0RCZmJpdmhYQzZZNUxT NTZwdz09IiwidlRhYiI6ImluZm8iLCJ2UGFnZSI6MSwiZ05hdiI6WyL-CoExhdGVzdCBWaWRlbyJdLCJnU2VjdCI6IkFMTClsImdQYWdlIjo-iMSIsInN5bSI6IiIsInNlYXJjaCI6IiJ9 (min 2:50)

84   Hal R. Arkes and Catherine Blumer, "The Psychology of Sunk Cost," *Organizational Behavior and Human Decision Processes* 35, 124-140 (1985), http://www.google.com/url?sa=t&rct=j&q=&esrc=s&sour ce=web&cd=1&sqi=2&ved=0CCUQFjAA&url=http%3A%2F%2Fcom monsenseatheism.com%2Fwp-content%2Fuploads%2F2011%2F09 %2FArkes-Blumer-The-psychology-of-sunk-cost.pdf&ei=Uy4cT8v1K dDsOci89JkL&usg=AFQjCNFE8XVozdwg8RW_kdmY2LfgvVMDZQ &sig2=2NzX5HvZjbct06MbtqPqXw

85   Richard McGill Murphy, "Why Doing Good Is Good for Business," *CNN Money* (February 2, 2010), money.cnn.com/2010/02/01/news/companies/dov_seidman_lrn.fortune/

86   CNN Wire Staff, "Tear gas flies during Chilean student protests," *CNN* (August 9, 2011), http://edition.cnn.com/2011/WORLD/americas/08/09/chile.protests/index.html

87   J. David Goodman, "At Least 80 Dead in Norway Shooting," *The New York Times* (July 22, 2011), http://www.nytimes.com/2011/07/23/world/europe/23oslo.html?pagewanted=all

88   Thomas L. Friedman, "A Theory of Everything (Sort Of)," *The York Times* (August 13, 2011), http://www.nytimes.com/2011/08/14/opinion/sunday/Friedman-a-theory-of-everyting-sort-of.html?_r=1

89   David W. Johnson and Roger T. Johnson, "An Educational Psychology Success Story: Social Interdependence Theory and Cooperative Learning," *Educational Researcher* 38 (2009): 365, doi: 10.3102/0013189X09339057

90   Nouriel Roubini, "ROUBINI: Ignore The Recent Economic Data — There's Still More Than A 50% Chance Of Recession," *Bussiness Insider* (October 25, 2011), http://articles.businessinsider.com/2011-10-25/markets/30318837_1_double-dip-recession-eurozone-ecri

91   "Short films from the 2011 Lindau Nobel Laureate Meeting in Economic Sciences," *The New Palgrave Dictionary of Economics Online*, http://www.dictionaryofeconomics.com/resources/news_lindau_meeting (the above-mentioned statement is in Stiglitz's video after 10:05 minutes.)

92   Amiel Ungar, "Polish Finance Minister Warns of War if EU Col-
      lapses," *Arutz Sheva* (September 16, 2011), http://www.israelnation-
      alnews.com/News/News.aspx/147945#.TrUbyPSArqE

93   Sebastian Boyd, "Chilean Peso Advances After Merkel Urges Fire-
      wall Around Greece," *Bloomberg* (September 26, 2011), http://www.
      businessweek.com/news/2011-09-26/chilean-peso-advances-after-
      merkel-urges-firewall-around-greece.html

94   Simon Kennedy, Rich Miller and Gabi Thesing, "Pimco sees Europe
      sliding into recession," *Financial Post* (September 26, 2011), http://
      business.financialpost.com/2011/09/26/pimco-sees-europe-sliding-
      into-recession/

95   Daniel Woolls, "Spain's Unemployment Rate Hits New Eurozone
      Record Of 21.3 Percent," *Huffington Post* (April 29, 2011), http://
      www.huffingtonpost.com/2011/04/29/span-unemployment-inflation-
      economy-debt_n_855341.html

96   United States Department of Labor, Bureau of Labor Statistics,
      www.bls.gov/news.release/empsit.nr0.htm

97   Perhaps the most notable examples are the studies published in the
      book, *Connected: The Surprising Power of Our Social Networks and
      How They Shape Our Lives—How Your Friends' Friends' Friends
      Affect Everything You Feel, Think, and Do*, by Dr. Nicholas A. Chris-
      takis and Prof. James Fowler:

      • Christakis, N. A.; Fowler, JH (22 May 2008). "The Collective
        Dynamics of Smoking in a Large Social Network" (PDF). *New
        England Journal of Medicine* 358 (21): 2249–2258.

      • Christakis, N. A.; Fowler, JH (26 July 2007). "The Spread of Obe-
        sity in a Large Social Network Over 32 Years" (PDF). *New England
        Journal of Medicine* 357 (4): 370–379

      • Fowler, J. H.; Christakis, N. A (3 January 2009). "Dynamic Spread
        of Happiness in a Large Social Network: Longitudinal Analysis
        Over 20 Years in the Framingham Heart Study" (PDF). *British
        Medical Journal* 337 (768): a2338.doi:10.1136/bmj.a2338. PMC
        2600606. PMID 19056788.

      • Christakis, N. A.; Fowler, JH (26 July 2007). "The Spread of Obe-
        sity in a Large Social Network Over 32 Years" (PDF). *New England
        Journal of Medicine* 357 (4): 370–379

98   "Average credit card debt per household with credit card debt:
      $15,799." By: Ben Woolsey and Matt Schulz, "Credit card statistics,
      industry facts, debt statistics," *CreditCards.com*, http://www.cred-

itcards.com/credit-card-news/credit-card-industry-facts-personal-debt-statistics-1276.php#Credit-card-debt

99 "The average British adult already owes £29,500, about 123 per cent of average earnings." By: Jeff Randall, "The debt trap time bomb," *The Telegraph* (October 31, 2011), http://www.telegraph.co.uk/finance/comment/jeffrandall/8859082/The-debt-trap-time-bomb.html

100 Ramy Inocencio, "World wastes 30% of all food," *CNN Business 360* (May 13, 2011), http://business.blogs.cnn.com/2011/05/13/30-of-all-worlds-food-goes-to-waste/

101 Tay, L., & Diener, E., "Needs and subjective well-being around the world," *Journal of Personality and Social Psychology* (2011), 101(2), 354-365. doi:10.1037/a0023779

102 "Education," *Encyclopædia Britannica*, http://www.britannica.com/EBchecked/topic/179408/education

103 Probably the most notable example of the influence of the social environment on our psyche and even our physical well-being is the book, *Connected: The Surprising Power of Our Social Networks and How They Shape Our Lives – How Your Friends' Friends' Friends Affect Everything You Feel, Think, and Do*, by Nicholas A. Christakis, MD, PhD, and James H. Fowler, PhD (Little, Brown and Co., 2010).

FURTHER READING

The Psychology of the Integral Society

The Psychology of the Integral Society presents a revolutionary approach to education. In an interconnected and interdependent world, teaching children to compete with their peers is as "wise" as teaching one's left hand to outsmart the right hand. An integral society is one in which all the parts contribute to the well-being and success of society. Society, in turn, is responsible for the well-being and success of those within it, thus forming interdependence. In a globalized, integrated world, this is the only sensible and *sustainable* way to live.

In this book, a series of dialogs between professors Michael Laitman and Anatoly Ulianov sheds light on the principles of an eye-opening approach to education. Absence of competition, child rearing through the social environment, peer equality, rewarding the givers, and a dynamic makeup of group and instructors are only some of the new concepts introduced in this book. *The Psychology of the Integral Society* is a must-have for all who wish to become better parents, better teachers, and better persons in the integrated reality of the 21ˢᵗ century.

> "What's expressed in *The Psychology of the Integral Society* should get people thinking about other possibilities. In solving any difficult problem, all perspectives need to be explored. We spend so much time competing and trying to get a leg up that the concept of simply working together sounds groundbreaking in itself."
>
> Peter Croatto, *ForeWord Magazine*

The Benefits of the New Economy:
Resolving the global economic crisis through mutual guarantee

Have you ever wondered why, for all the efforts of the best economists in the world, the economic crisis refuses to wane? The answer to that question lies with us, all of us. The economy is a reflection of our relationships. Through natural development, the world has become an integrated global village where we are all interdependent.

Interdependence and "globalization" mean that what happens in one part of the world affects every other part of it. As a result, a solution to the global crisis must include the whole world, for if only one part of it is healed, other, still ailing parts, will make it ill again.

The Benefits of the New Economy was written out of concern for our common future. Its purpose is to improve our understanding of today's economic turmoil—its causes, how it can be solved, and its anticipated outcome. The road toward a new economy lies not in levying new taxes, printing money, or in any remedy from the past. Rather, the solution lies with a society where all support each other in mutual guarantee. This creates a social environment of care and consideration, and the understanding that we will rise or fall together, because we are all interdependent.

This book contains thirteen "standalone" essays written in 2011 by several economists and financiers from different disciplines. Each essay addresses a specific issue, and can be read as a separate unit. However, one theme connects them: the absence of mutual guarantee as the cause of our problems in the global-integral world.

You can read these essays in an order of your choice. We, the authors, believe that if you read at least several essays you will receive a more comprehensive view of the required transformation in order to resolve the global crisis and create a sustainable, prosperous economy.

ABOUT THE ARI INSTITUTE

MISSION STATEMENT

The Advanced Research of Integration (ARI) Institute is a 501(c)(3) nonprofit organization dedicated to promoting positive changes in educational policies and practices through innovative ideas and solutions. These can be applied to the most pressing educational issues of our time. The ARI Institute introduces a new way of thinking by explaining the benefits of recognizing and implementing the new rules humanity needs to succeed in an interdependent, integrated world.

Through its networks, activities and multimedia resources, ARI Institute promotes international and interdisciplinary cooperation.

WHAT WE DO

We encourage active dialogue on the global crisis as an opportunity to facilitate a positive shift in global thinking about educating future generations, thus enabling them to cope with massive shifts in climate, economics, and geopolitical relations. Our materials are free and available to all, regardless of age, gender, religion, political, or cultural considerations.

The materials reveal the integral, global system of natural laws manifesting in society today. We are committed to sharing our knowledge on an international level through our established multimedia channels. We are further committed to enhancing people's awareness of the need to conduct their relations in a spirit of mutual responsibility and personal involvement.

OUR VALUES

We are all living in trying times, confronted by personal, environmental, and social crises. These crises are occurring because humankind has been unable to perceive the interconnectedness and interdependence among us and between the human race and Nature. By providing information to the public through a rich media environment, we act as a catalyst to shift human behavior toward a more sustainable model. We advocate a solution to the current global crisis and promote it through our unique educational content, presented via media channels worldwide.

Through extensive research and public activities, ARI Institute offers a clear, coherent understanding of the natural development of the events and societal degradation that have led to the current state of affairs in our global, integral world. Additionally, we are expanding our online environment to reach children. They will benefit by participating in an educational process that encourages them to become tolerant, responsible, and considerate human beings living as global citizens.

In this internet-based environment, children will collaborate in activities simultaneously occurring in different parts of the world. Such activities will help them recognize that they are all connected within a united global village, and show them how they can help improve humanity by participating in these programs. We believe that exposure to this environment can profoundly change an entire generation of children, turning them into responsible citizens of the world, and marking a turning point in humankind's currently destructive behaviors.

WHERE WE STAND ON EDUCATION

The new generation is facing a completely new world filled with unprecedented challenges. If we focus on our children's needs, we can significantly help them face problems such as drug abuse, violence, and increasing school dropout rates, issues that we believe are not being successfully addressed by most current educational systems.

WHERE WE STAND ON ECONOMICS

The crisis is neither financial nor economic, nor is it ecological. Rather, it is a global crisis that encompasses our entire civilization and all realms of life. Therefore, we must look at the root of it and address the common cause—our self-centered nature.

We believe that a superficial change in society will not yield a lasting solution. First, we must alter the connections between us, moving from egocentrism to altruism. This is the principle by which integral systems operate, and today we are discovering that human society is precisely such a system.

OUR ACTIVITIES

TV and Video Productions
ARI Films (www.arifilms.tv) is ARI's film and television department, a highly successful, dynamic production enterprise specializing in content for the Internet, cable, and satellite television stations. ARI Films produces educational and documentary programs, docudramas, and talk show series, as well as custom made productions. The ARI Films team consists of experienced professionals from a wide array of fields including video editors, animators, cameramen, scriptwriters, producers and directors.

International Forums
ARI organizes regular international forums all over the world that are attended by large audiences eager to participate in its lectures and workshops. These forums are broadcast live over the internet and on cable and satellite TV networks.

The Citizens of the Future:
Our Education Center and Network
Citizens of the Future is a not-for-profit educational association established under the auspices of ARI. It aims to provide children, youth, and parents with an online learning environment that promotes values of love and caring for others, so vital in this global age. We believe

that children who acquire and adhere to these values will be well positioned for a life of happiness, joy, and self-fulfillment. To achieve its goals, the Citizens of the Future association operates on several levels, as listed below.

Network of Children's Education Centers

Citizens of the Future education centers are places where the method of "building human beings" is developed and implemented on a daily basis. Here, a loving and supportive environment is constructed in favor of the children, based on friendship and care for each other. The activities include:

- Activities and games that promote bonding among the children;

- Discussions about Nature in general and human nature in particular;

- Complementary lessons on various school topics;

- Developing the necessary social skills for interpersonal and group communication;

- Outings to museums, parks, nature reserves, courthouses, and many more locations and facilities that help introduce the children to the systems that affect our lives;

- Documentation of activities and preparation of structured tutorials for instructors to circulate this innovative method worldwide.

YFU YOUTH MOVEMENT

The youth movement, YFU (Youth For Unity), was specifically formed to create a supportive, loving environment for youths from 12-18 who aspire to promote the values of mutual consideration and love of others. This social framework is a direct extension of the complementary education center, Citizens of the Future. Activities of YFU include:

- Studies of Nature in general and human nature in particular;

- Professional training;

- Cinema school;

- Conventions, trips, and other unity-promoting activities;

- Tutoring and training of children, to qualify the next generation for life in an interconnected world;

- Preparation and guidance for life as adults in today's world;

- Developing lesson plans on love of others, human nature, and Nature as a whole;

- Production and distribution of children's programs and programs on education;

- Developing educational games;

- Organizing conventions for children, parents, and educators.

ABOUT DR. MICHAEL LAITMAN, FOUNDER OF THE ARI INSTITUTE

Dr. Laitman is the highly qualified founder of the ARI Institute. He holds degrees as Professor of Ontology and Theory of Knowledge, a PhD in Philosophy, and an MS in Medical Cybernetics. Today, the ARI Institute has branches throughout North America, Central and South America, as well as Asia, Africa, and Western and Eastern Europe.

Dr. Laitman is dedicated to discovering and promoting positive changes in educational policies and practices, and applying them to the most pressing educational problems of our time. He proposes a new approach to education that implements the rules of living in an interdependent, integrated world.

A Guide to Living in a Globalized World

Dr. Laitman provides specific guidelines for how to live in the new global village, our increasingly technologically interconnected world. His fresh perspective touches all areas of human life: social, economic, and environmental, with a particular emphasis on education. He outlines a new global education system based on universal values. This would create a cohesive society in our emerging, more tightly interconnected reality.

In his meetings with Mrs. Irina Bokova, Director-General of UNESCO, and with Dr. Asha-Rose Migiro, Deputy Secretary-General of the UN, he discussed current worldwide education problems and his vision for their solution. This crucial topic is presently in the process of major transformation. Dr. Laitman stresses the urgency of taking advantage of newly available communication tools, while considering the unique aspirations of today's youth and preparing them for life in a highly dynamic, global world.

In recent years Dr. Laitman has worked closely with many international institutions and has participated in several international events in Tokyo with the Goi Peace Foundation, Arosa (Switzerland), and Düsseldorf (Germany), and with the International Forum of Cultures in Monterrey (Mexico). These events were organized with the support of UNESCO. In these global forums, he contributed to vital discussions concerning the world crisis, and outlined the steps required to create positive change through an enhanced global awareness.

Dr. Laitman has been featured in international media, including *Corriere della Sera*, the *Chicago Tribune*, the *Miami Herald*, *The Jerusalem Post*, and *The Globe* and on RAI TV and Bloomberg TV.

He has devoted his life to exploring human nature and society, seeking answers to the meaning of life in our modern world. The combination of his academic background and extensive knowledge make him a sought-after world thinker and speaker. Dr. Laitman has written over 40 books that have been translated into 18 languages, all with the goal of helping individuals achieve harmony among them and with the environment around them.

Dr. Laitman's scientific approach allows people of all backgrounds, nationalities, and faiths to rise above their differences and unite around the global message of mutual responsibility and collaboration.

CONTACT INFORMATION

Inquiries and general information:
info@ariresearch.org

USA
2009 85th St., Suite 51
Brooklyn NY, USA -11214
Tel. +1-917-6284343

Canada
1057 Steeles Avenue West
Suite 532
Toronto, ON – M2R 3X1 Canada
Tel. +1 416 274 7287

Israel
112 Jabotinsky St.,
Petach Tikva, 49517 Israel
i.vinokur@ariresearch.org
Tel. +972-545606780